Copyright © 2022 Tekkan
Artwork Copyright © 2022

All rights reserved.
First Printing, 2022
ISBN 978-1-7363537-9-0

To contact Tekkan please email:
buddhaboy1289@gmail.com

Table of Contents

Book I . . . . .Page 1

Portrait . . . . Page 1

John Henry . . . . Page 2

Tyrannosaurus *in Requiem* . . . . .Page 3

Book II . . . . Page 101

Book III . . . . Page 201

of . . . . Page 295

Book IV . . . . Page 301

Rest in Peace Mike Finley . . . . .Page 310

Book V. . . . . Page 401

Thic Nhat Hanh. . . . . .Page 439

Thirty-eight Years Ago . . . . . . .Page 452

Edward Scissorhands . . . . Page 479

How to Read My Poems

I want to be direct in my meaning — I want people to clearly understand my meaning. My wordiness is inspired by Shakespeare, and the (aimed-for) concision is in imitation of Japanese style. Using the sonnet with the tanka, I mix the sensibility of the Occident and the Orient — which I have done by living in England, Japan, and America.

I have married the sonnet to the tanka. I tell a story in the sonnet. The story builds to a conclusion in the last line. The tanka is a commentary, or a counterpoint, to the sonnet — the combined poems have two endings.

Recently I have added limericks and doggerel into my repertoire. The limericks have a rhyme scheme but the tanka do not.

I don't punctuate much in my poetry. I want the words themselves to do the work. There is logic between words, and the forms provide structure. By not using punctuation I hope to direct readers to carefully attend to each word — to appreciate the graininess of words.

Reading my poems silently and reading them aloud may be different experiences. There's not always a pause intended at the end of the line.

Hint: *sonnets are to be recited not as lines but as phrases, and a phrase often overflows the break at the end of a line. I pause and take a breath where it seems natural for me to pause. Another person may pause differently than I do.*

Each poem is a piece of a mosaic, and it is my hope that the collection of poems forms a portrait of consciousness.

My friend, *Will Ersland*, is a wonderful artist. His paintings grace book. My daughter, *Jocelyn Figueroa*, is also a wonderful artist. Her fish charms page 154.

I am Barry MacDonald. I received the *dharma* name *Tekkan*, which means "Iron Man," a settled practitioner of great determination.

— *Tekkan*

Book I

Portrait

She smiles with ease, as lovely as a child;
And like a child she laughs with simple joys,
As though a candle's radiance were wild
Enough and life and love and men were toys.
Her girlish blush is coy and innocent,
Her slender form displays her elegance,
Her shoulder's curve is slim and delicate,
And all her movements sketch a feline grace.
Why does her beauty spark so much unrest?
How may her innocence exact such shame?
When she is near my loneliness has rest,
And love's seduction seems a harmless game.
But she contrives her lovely smile with ease,
And all her dear affections only tease.

(Written in 1983.)

John Henry

Another morning sun will sear the air —
Such humidity. The whole body aches.
To rise again to labor hard will tear
Muscles from sinews. The tired body quakes.
Shades don't cool the blazing of the noon sun.
Within a soul a fury wakes to coil
A wrath to hurl the maul to powder tons
Of stone to hide a shame in deadly toil.
Evening glows with the grace of sunset's rose.
At twilight the sweat dries in salty cakes
Across those huge slumped shoulders and he dozes
As he stumbles as he trudges as he aches.
He dreams of mountains cold rivers and lakes —
The earth is so beautiful that he aches.

(Written in 1983.)

Bald-pated Tyrannosaur you can't catch me
You may lumber and roar and crush a car
You may snarl with your teeth like scimitars
You stomp and blunder but can't bite me
You may shake your head but you can't get me
You may very well be the king of beasts
With every creature comprising a feast
You rule the forest but can't swallow me
With all your majesty you can't touch me
You may trot and gambol and have a ball
You stomp and smash and rip and tear and maul
But whatever you do you can't catch me
And wherever you go you won't see me
Because you are now extinct don't you see?

Tyrannosaurs *in Requiem*

He gamboled upon the earth
He expressed plenty of mirth
But he's had his day
And it's fair to say
He won't have another birth.

P.S. a tyrannosaur may crush cars —
in the movies.

It's 2 a.m. and the cat wants to play
As he is gamboling upon my bed
Pouncing and biting until I say "hey
It's way too early and you have been fed"
As I'm feeling the pulsation of blood
Throbbing at my temples on the pillow
And Kitcat jumps to the floor with a thud
And what he thinks he's doing yes I know
Because I've gotten him used to playing
When I will rise from bed before the dawn
When I brush and rub him while I'm singing
When he loves his brushing and has his fun
When he gets excited and wants to fight
When I slap his paws and he tries to bite.

Kitcat had reason
to think I was getting up
from sleeping because
I rose from bed twice
to write notes for a poem.

The indigo bunting migrates at night
Following stars for orientation
Adjusting the angle guiding its flight
Taking its bearings from constellations
The brilliant bluest blue of all the birds
Its feathers refract and reflect the light
Its beauty far surpasses all my words
Seeing it suddenly is a delight
The birds will return sometime within May
To flit and frolic on the edge of woods
But its image is helping me today
To overcome my frigid winter moods
The birds nest in roadside thickets fields streams
They also resonate in winter dreams.

February snow
minutely sparkles with
the brightest sunlight
but eventually I
get tired of seeing the snow.

I think today is Super Bowl Sunday
And by quickly perusing with Google
I learn the Kansas City Chiefs will play
The Tampa Bay Buccaneers for boodle
Forty years ago I did like football
My team was the Minnesota Vikings
The Purple People Eaters stood so tall
They destroyed the offense with me cheering
The Vikings went to the Super Bowl twice
And I was enamored and excited
But twice they were humbled like little mice
And I was depressed and disappointed
I think sometimes if the Vikings had won
My entire life would have been more fun.

The Vikings lost not
twice but four times at the
Super Bowl and I
was crushed and haven't watched an
hour of football ever since.

The Northern Cardinal doesn't migrate
It fluffs its feathers and endures the cold
In February its calls will vibrate
As the mating of the male becomes bold
Fluttering swooping gliding it appears
A scarlet flash amid the pristine snow
A loveliness of red and white cohere
In an instant a marvelous tableau
A cardinal in winter is a gift
In the middle of a frigid season
Hungry and scavenging it must persist
It is beautiful without a reason
It's exceedingly odd the way things are
That such beauty exists is quite bizarre.

Latent energy
lies dormant inside of the
gnarly contorted
branches of a winter tree
as a cardinal perches.

My head is exhausted so I'm quitting
Scrounging for words is a dreary business
Working so hard while stoically sitting
Fussing with syllables is an illness
Attempting to rhyme contorts the grammar
Very often the meaning makes no sense
Pounding out rhymes with a ball peen hammer
Waiting for ideas creates suspense
I've had too much coffee now I'm weary
My acuity is out the window
I really do want to take it easy
All I can do now is mumbo-jumbo
I am very tired and it's time to quit
Don't especially care if words don't fit.

It is such a waste of time
Straining and trying to rhyme
They're kind of a crutch
They don't mean much
And the poems aren't worth a dime.

Sometimes I remember my old mentor
Cid Corman pronouncing that rhyme is dead
It's antiquated and lost its vigor
It's much better to speak freely instead
As language isn't so artificial
And resists being tied with pretty bows
The meaning with rhymes is superficial
Poetry becomes vainglorious pose
And rhyming sounds like pontification
The consequence of a fragile ego
It's better to go for self-negation
To exhibit oneself incognito
But is rhyme really dead — maybe not yet
I guess it all depends on a mindset.

It's not very hard to rhyme
And it doesn't take much time
Just type in a word
At RhymeZone.com
And find a rhyme anytime.

Our society is having a purge
Of the menace White Supremacy
So that justice will finally emerge
We have a problem with our history
Because we honor mendacious people
We must destroy statues and monuments
To create a benevolent sequel
The downtrodden will gain predominance
White women are not deserving of blame
But the white Christian men are the problem
We must make propitious use of shame
And follow the path of Joseph Stalin
Historical white men must disappear
And it's time to cancel William Shakespeare.

Shakespeare is just a big dope
Let's get ahold of a rope
We'll circle his head
So he can drop dead
And we can inspire hope.

While waiting for a train in Amsterdam
On the ferry of the English Channel
Thinking about his poems on a tram
Visiting his gravesite in a chapel
I appreciated Shakespeare's sonnets
And adored his Elizabethan pomp
He was quite lovesick and I believed it
Inspiring an ethereal whomp
His verbiage is like thick molasses
With clever rhymes and opal metaphors
He gave vent to superlative passions
Not getting enough and wanting much more
Each of Shakespeare's sonnets is a puzzle
Lyrical exorbitant and subtle.

But I don't know why
anyone would rhyme like that
it's kind of crazy
this Houdini trick with words
is just piffle for the birds.

There are things to do in a sudden thaw
Without a smidgeon of hesitation
It's like an ecclesiastical law
And to waste time is a violation
I race to the carwash and wait in line
Because the car is badly encrusted
As the snowplows spew a god-awful brine
And I refuse to let the car be rusted
So I will loiter with the radio
Snug like a bug in a rug in my car
Savoring the frothy sudsy gizmo
And afterward I can grin like a rock star
As life is so brief I do need to act
And enjoy more than my digestive tract.

I patiently wait my turn
Past the point of no return
I can't move an inch
I'm starting to itch
My heart's beginning to burn.

The blanket of snow won't be here for long
It's covered in rabbit and squirrel prints
As much milder days are coming along
But now there are innumerable glints
With sunlight sparking millions of crystals
Their fire is refracting in pinpoint jewels
Becoming sharp iridescent pixels
But quickly this snow will melt into pools
Clouds are making a high thin ceiling
Moving gradually within the sky
But even with the clouds it's revealing
The potency of light will multiply
Spring is approaching and the snow will go
And I will warm myself — like a tomato.

The red squirrel is busy
Running on top of the fence
He stops and he runs
He runs and he stops
Making perfect squirrel sense.

I do admit it isn't really fair
To compare my poems with what they did
It is easy now because of software
While they depended so much upon id
When weary I turn to a thesaurus
When rhyming I go to RhymeZone.com
To find a partner with "polymorphous"
And thereby poetizing with aplomb
But old-time poets relied on their heads
They couldn't surf the web for verbiage
They exhausted their gray matter instead
And they must have mustered so much courage
But I don't care and I am quite happy
That I can rhyme and make it sound snappy.

I come to my desk and sit
Hunting for a rhyme that fits
It's not for acclaim
It's only a game
Choosing a "banana split."

I do like my experiments with rhyme
It's not difficult and just takes practice
But I won't be doing it all of the time
To make it a habit would be madness
It's kind of crazy and not normal speech
It could easily be illogical
To rhyme formally is to sort of preach
And perhaps it is pathological
But just for a lark I would love to see
The president give special emphasis
And concoct a brand-new style by maybe
Rhyming the State of the Union Address
I would love to see that bunch of dummies
Sit and listen as it would be funny.

The president is stoic
He lives by the Potomac
Better than normal
Because he's formal
The president's heroic.

Rhyming sonnets is an amusing game
As long as I admit they don't mean much
It's fun and maybe just a little lame
Even as the habit could be a crutch
Finding blustery words is a puzzle
Striking a pretentious poetic pose
Stirring up drama tempo and sizzle
And finishing with effortless repose
Surely the poet has sincerity
There's no purpose to writing otherwise
Just a useless verbal dexterity
But sometimes it's good to spring a surprise
I could put this sonnet on my tombstone
To inspire a laugh and not a moan.

Here lies Barry cold and dead
Without a thought in his head
He found clarity
And hilarity
With not a word left unsaid.

Snow will be melting in the next two weeks
All the walkways and roads will be a mess
And overnight so much water will freeze
So I walk with more than a little stress
As thin ice is almost invisible
So it's important to be clearheaded
Spotting a glint of ice is pivotal
Because I am not very hardheaded
And don't want to give my noggin a whack
It takes an instant of inattention
And more than my head could suffer a crack
I dread the tears of hyperextension
There are many perils that come with spring
And I don't want to see my legs upswing.

A moment's inattention
Means discombobulation
Involving a whack
Of a hard impact
And then incomprehension.

I am not deceived by appearances
I know all the snow is on the way out
But I don't forget my old grievances
I know what "spring melt" is really about
It is fabulous within a few days
Winter's accumulated snow will go
As the sun is marvelously ablaze
And the grass may even begin to grow
But it's a deception I've seen before
It seems the blizzards are finally gone
I don't have to wear big boots anymore
But it's a trick and I'm not a moron
It's a certainty in Minnesota
April blizzards are part of a quota.

The warmth is all very fine
And I enjoy the sunshine
It's no time for fun
Because we're not done
It will snow multiple times.

In politics it is easy to lose
There is an art in prevaricating
It is beneficial to skew the news
So many events are irritating
The politicos know how to accuse
Shaping the narrative is important
It is a trick to confuse and abuse
Being honorable is impotent
To rise in the ranks they follow their cues
The system becomes a nasty machine
Originality they won't excuse
The exercise of force is often mean
Most Americans haven't got a clue
They are being deceived — I wish they knew.

He is honest he is bold
His virtue will not be sold
His integrity
And sincerity
Are a beauty to behold.

Give me the company of desperate
Drunks who are struggling to be sober
To drink is to die and they accept it
The forgetful bliss they had is over
The chaos they create is dangerous
They grieve their families and they know it
And then driving while drunk is treacherous
They have compulsion and can't control it
They need to talk to the people like them
They are confused and need to express it
They are terrified of the days to come
The urge is tempting but they repress it
And their loneliness is hard to fathom
It's necessary to hit rock bottom.

An alcoholic
has no control over how
much he drinks once he
starts again and no control
over the consequences.

The scorn he gets is understandable
There is not an easy explanation
The damage is incomprehensible
Apologies prompt exasperation
And the alcoholic is pathetic
Why on earth he can't stop is the question
And quite often he seems apathetic
He's not even open to suggestions
Or he's mournful and apologetic
And expresses the best of intentions
But it is hard to be sympathetic
He's not a person who learns his lessons
His drunken antics are deplorable
Living with him becomes unbearable.

He doesn't know why
he does what he does — even
the hangovers are
not enough to curtail an
inevitable binge.

So how does one help an alcoholic?
Relinquishing control is the first step
Repeating behavior is neurotic
And making excuses is a misstep
He has to hit bottom to get better
He has to suffer the consequences
The more pain he feels — so much the better
He needs to be stripped of his defenses
Coddling or soothing doesn't help him
Keep him from driving when drunk if you can
Call the police and let them arrest him
Let him suffer more pain than he can stand
His hitting rock bottom is essential
This isn't cruel — it is consequential.

There are circles of
sober alcoholics he
can join to gain the
communication and the
knowledge of recovery.

I understand them because I am one
And did get sober many years ago
What alcoholics do is what I've done
There are meetings and steps to undergo
Self-loathing isn't a permanent state
I've earned my freedom and my confidence
I learned how to pray and to meditate
And uncover the snares of consciousness
The hopeless desperation is a gift
A metamorphosis is possible
To perceive differently is a lift
To balance emotion is plausible
I don't live at all like I did before
And am not self-destructive anymore.

Thoughts and emotions
need not be weightier than
the clouds in the sky
if I can let go of them
then that is liberation.

The distant horizon is salmon pink
I have always loved watching the sunrise
Something about it forces me to think
It's more than a festival for my eyes
The trees are beautiful black silhouettes
Making a worthy foreground for the sky
There is a magic that we all possess
The power of consciousness in disguise
Intellect and emotions coalesce
Sensuous exploration clarifies
In meditation being may fluoresce
Disruptive circumstances harmonize
As the uprising sun may crystallize
There is a depth in peace to realize.

The moon is on
a different angle than
the spinning earth
as the moon shines before dawn
and after the sun rises.

I want to play and be spontaneous
I'm not aiming to be nasty or lie
I'd like to winnow what's extraneous
To empower me to hit the bullseye
My topics are contemporaneous
Some people are angry but I stand by
All kerfuffle is simultaneous
So many grievances do multiply
And opinions are miscellaneous
I am only an ordinary guy
But the sunrise is momentaneous
I'm not sure I'm making sense — but I try
And it is worthy to be conscientious
I'm not sure it's possible — I can't lie.

Dr. Seuss wrote children's books
He wrote funny rhyming hooks
Thing One and Thing Two
They matter to you
We all love his storybooks.

The trick in life is to be lovable
The trap to avoid is rigidity
Love is happiness love is flammable
It consumes the heart with rapidity
It's most helpful to be adaptable
Be like water possess fluidity
No one's perfect we all are fallible
To condemn yourself is stupidity
And to make mistakes is acceptable
Meditation offers lucidity
So much of the world can be magical
Be enlightened with pellucidity
There's more to life than being logical
Find wisdom in the mythological.

I start my day with my cat
And every morning we chat
We wrestle and fight
And he tries to bite
We have a playful combat.

I don't want to be ceremonial
I'd like to think I have sincerity
I favor words that are colloquial
Without descending to vulgarity
It's not hard to be sanctimonial
With a scornful familiarity
But it's more playful to be jovial
Being deceitful is barbarity
To utter jargon would be provincial
I want joyful conviviality
The meaning should be unmistakable
A lightning bolt comes from temerity
With an added touch of hilarity.

God help me I'm liking it
Looking for the rhymes that fit
I sit on my butt
And create rut
Being a silly nitwit.

The patter of words is delectable
And the lines are a pleasure to compose
The easier words are more digestible
And then they may topple like dominoes
Sometimes my manner is questionable
Being mischievous I won't foreclose
A sly subtlety is detectable
As every new line will superimpose
It is horrid to be predictable
I keep in my pocket a yellow rose
Oh my habits are uncorrectable
I am a rascal right down to my toes
I am trying to be respectable
But the rhyming is too obsessional.

So often I am doing it
Can't really excuse it
It's a waste of time
Just trying to rhyme
Pretty soon I will stop it.

Each of my poems is a flirtation
In a way I'm saying "come play with me"
You don't have to — there's no obligation
But playing with words is my specialty
You don't need crafty sophistication
Poetry can be light and feathery
I don't harbor any expectations
But how many ways can we say "Whoopee"?
I won't pronounce fussy declarations
I won't be a scary mournful banshee
Having fun needs no justification
We can frolic like golden bumblebees
The words are more than mere decoration
They may inspire your liberation.

Let's try for simplicity
With happy complicity
We don't need bother
We won't use blather
We can have felicity.

It's difficult now and I don't know why
I'm much more frantic than I want to be
There is frustration but I will get by
Usually I have more energy
That is not true and I'd rather not lie
I am just not seizing my synergy
I've become an inarticulate guy
And not the poet that I'd like to be
My mind is awake but it won't comply
If the words don't flow then I'm not happy
I will calm myself and detoxify
And God keep me from becoming sloppy
I really have to try and simplify
It is my only chance to clarify.

Morning is my apogee
Morning is my jubilee
I rise with the sun
And then I have fun
Morning is my energy.

You don't have the time to fritter away
Don't allow cogitation to stultify
You must gather yourself and seize the day
You can't let your synapses ossify
The world's a festival — go out and play
Don't let your knees and elbows calcify
You may still vacation in Paraguay
Think of all the whimsy to gratify
Excite your companions host a soirée
Contact an old friend and reunify
You might even be a little risqué
You can't let epiphanies pass you by
Liberate anxiety with reggae
Enjoy Hemingway with café au lait.

Don't be sorry don't be blue
Get over that stomach flu
Life is savory
It's not slavery
Take a trip to Katmandu.

You are lucky you aren't a crustacean
Excuse me I don't mean to speechify
You need not listen to my dictation
Being human — what does that signify?
I say it's a cause for celebration
We have both arms and legs — do you know why?
I really enjoy my ambulation
And wouldn't want to be a tsetse fly
That would be such a humiliation
I can do subtractions and multiply
And contribute to civilization
I can classify and personify
Having fingers for manipulation
And a big brain for specification.

Doggerel isn't easy
As it needs to be breezy
It has to be fun
And turn on a pun
Even if it is cheesy.

The air isn't cold but is quite chilly
The overcast sky is a gloomy gray
But I am happy and even silly
I'm pretty sure it's going to rain all day
The snow is mostly gone and there's the grass
The frost is leaving and the soil is moist
Sure it's messy now but the rain will pass
Every year at this time I do rejoice
This is different than a winter day
The air is very damp and quite misty
The dry lip-splitting air has passed away
This kind of air makes metal things rusty
I know there will be snowy days to come
But now I see no reason to be glum.

The tumultuous
howling wind of the last few
days must have roused the
roots of the trees from slumber
to take minerals again.

I confess to a little negligence
I am supposed to be reading the news
But it's an insult to intelligence
And every day it's just a nasty ooze
It's full of opinion that I don't trust
Reporters are condescending and smug
Topics they cover are meant to disgust
But the overall impact makes me shrug
I'm sure the news is manipulative
News people present slanted opinions
They think their views are authoritative
They want to foist important decisions
Reading the news is a predicament
I take it in selective increments.

I like writing poetry
It's like psychotherapy
I do not scowl
I do not growl
Usually I'm happy.

I learn a lot from my metal dumbbell
It just lies on the floor so patiently
But it has the oomph to make me humble
And I can't lift it with complacency
As it weighs exactly 100 pounds
It takes my focus and it makes me strain
And I do struggle with the ups and downs
And the effort even squeezes my brain
I do have a fear of letting it go
Because my wrists aren't quite sturdy enough
I am terrified of smashing a toe
But absolutely I'm not giving up
Usually it's a hunk of metal
But its latent force is elemental.

It's not lovely it's not art
Doesn't really warm my heart
And my dumbbell
Doesn't ever smell
Though it often makes me fart.

To any amount determinable
Without any perception deleted
Even though perhaps unmanageable
Maybe so unusually gifted
Not excluding many obtrusive things
Including the imperceptibly small
Involving the physics theories of strings
Wanting it too much creates a pitfall
Sometimes an unavoidable nuisance
Resonating in a temple bell's gong
Encompassing desperate truculence
Also the unjustifiably wrong
You see enlightenment is everything
In partnership with a pregnant nothing.

It's not me who is
responsible for this
poem as I laid
my head upon my pillow
and words came from somewhere else.

The barren trees are swaying in the breeze
The grass is dry but it's not growing yet
It's warm today but it's kind of a tease
Spring is coming but it isn't here yet
Snow is approaching but there won't be much
There's no denying the sun's new dazzle
And snow will fall but I'm not caring much
As winter's grasp is becoming feeble
I'm looking forward to the bright fresh leaves
To the budding of the apple blossoms
I want to hear the wind tossing the leaves
I love crabapple and cherry blossoms
And it won't be long before we hear the frogs
The tree the chorus and the peeper frogs.

Spring leaves
in breezes
tumble
swell
soothe.

This could be a day in February
As it snowed last night and the sky is white
But the snow is only temporary
And most of it will be gone by tonight
I'm taking the time to enjoy the snow
As if I had never seen it before
Very soon the grass will begin to grow
And it won't be bitter cold anymore
The weight of winter is dissipating
I can feel a spring moisture in the air
Bright days are coming — I don't mind waiting
Gloom may be lingering but I don't care
So many winters have come and passed by
But I never tire of watching the sky.

Winter dissipating
river ice dissolving
birds and trees
grass and leaves
soon titillating.

Jason sees a gaggle of geese and swans
Flying together in one formation
Jason understands the geese and the swans
Not surprised by their cooperation
He strides through William O'Brien State Park
And it's exhausting for me to keep up
He points out the Neolithic landmarks
After eleven miles he speeds up
He tells me about the various trees
He sees flowers that don't look like flowers
He has a mastery of the species
As I stride stomp and struggle for hours
Afterwards I know much more than I did
And my feet are aching and I'm done in.

For Jason every
season is not merely a
repetition of
of previous seasons but
a new origination.

The wiener dog has pomp and dignity
It's not concerned about your opinion
In its own way it displays symmetry
It's not a dog of easy submission
The dachshund is intelligent and bold
Bred by the Germans for hunting badgers
Its trotting style is a sight to behold
And the dog has a mouth full of daggers
It is long of body and short of leg
The carriage of its head shows confidence
With strangers it may be a powder keg
It has an appetite that's bottomless
And the dog may beg with very sad eyes
But tossing it table scraps is unwise.

The wiener dog is sporty
The wiener dog is snippy
its trotting along
is worthy of song
The wiener dog is perky.

Maybe it's better to be ignorant
And ignore political opinion
To slide by and become indifferent
And avoid the difficult decisions
But I'm not passive and I care too much
That politics today is dangerous
I'd like to discourse with a feather's touch
But so many topics are treacherous
We are spoon-fed nonstop accusation
Politicos purposely polarize
They profit from flammable gyrations
They hone their messages to demonize
The media is used to hypnotize
With the cruel intention to brutalize.

Lawyers and judges
law enforcement bureaucrats
the educators
and the media people
are all bitter partisans.

The issues are like Russian nesting dolls
Each of the dolls appears differently
A difference in knowledge makes a wall
Without knowledge there is no sympathy
The biggest doll is the news narrative
Partisan journalism isn't true
News is emotional and addictive
There is much dishonesty to sort through
Each doll presents greater complexity
The range of opinion is tremendous
Involving the context and history
And a lively debate could be endless
But the smallest doll is about power
And the truth about politics is sour.

Rules for Radicals
by Saul Alinsky and
The Prince
by Machiavelli
reveal the various tricks.

What do we mean when we say "consciousness"?
Does it include what we do while sleeping?
Is it just a measure of thoughtfulness?
Does everything have it if it's living?
I look at turkey vultures and eagles
Watching how they drift and soar with the wind
I listen to the mournful calls of gulls
Are they outside or inside of my mind?
I do some things of which I'm not aware
I am breathing lungs and beating a heart
Circulating blood and growing my hair
Am I one with the earth or set apart?
There is the weightiness of emotions
As imponderable as the oceans.

Do I separate
what happens
from how I respond?

A surge of power presses my body
As the engines roar along the runway
Speed is intensifying mightily
As the weight of my body falls away
As the airliner's wheels are lifting off
A thrust of power is precipitous
The plane is ascending steeply aloft
The engine's roaring is continuous
Pressure on my ears is making them pop
Something feels different but I'm not sure what
I'm feeling the blood in my temples throb
My seatbelt is locked and I'm staying put
The view from the window is amazing
The earth far below the clouds is moving.

Stuck in my seat
I'm reading a novel
waiting patiently
for a bottle of water
almonds and a biscuit.

The wind is taking me in sudden bursts
Testing the balance of the bicycle
It comes in roaring overwhelming spurts
But I can make it more manageable
I have to tame my appetite for speed
Because the wind is much stronger than me
Setting a gentle pace is what I need
The motion is easy and I'm carefree
It's exciting with the wind at my back
Now I'm speeding as fast as a greyhound
The time passes quickly and I lose track
My animal spirit is quite unbound
Spring is coming and the trees are budding
Today is joyous — the sunlight stunning.

The rippling river
far below the bridge
reflects sky and clouds —
the wind batters me
and the gulls.

It's easy to miss how lucky we are
Just stare at the news to become depressed
The propaganda they push is bizarre
Consume too much and you will be confused
Indulging anger is a sad mistake
I know because I've done it quite often
Resentment produces only heartache
I'd rather my emotions be softened
There is a vast world beyond my thinking
Occasionally I holiday there
Spring is coming and the trees are waking
And jubilant birdsong is in the air
Thought follows thought follows thought —
It's so easy to get tied up in knots.

Breath follows
breath follows
breath — it's
a better rhythm
to attend to.

It's April 1st and I'm feeling lazy
The snow is all gone and the sky is blue
Playing with words is a little crazy
I am sure there's something better to do
It's too chilly to ride my bicycle
I'm at my desk looking out my window
Just doing nothing isn't radical
It is better than playing pachinko
Oh well I lost a girlfriend poor poor me
I am just too weary to change her mind
There are advantages to being free
I can play with words if I'm so inclined
There are parts of me I don't want to change
So it's a better deal to disengage.

I am lackadaisical
with love drifting along
listening to bird song
too lazy to
move.

Let's have fun with innocent malaprops
I want to dance with you the flamingo
Let's have popcorn and watch an agitprop
A most lovely bird is the flamenco
The English language is full of riddles
The same vowels are spelled so differently
My handwriting is an awful scribble
I'm not capable of calligraphy
As I kid I was inarticulate
No one's ideal of virtuosity
I wasn't suspected of intelligence
And had not a hint of verbosity
But now I am old and full of whimsy
Don't give a damn — and my ego's flimsy.

Trouble comes from
being serious —
nonsense is
easy.

I would like my mind to be like a bowl
And to accept with grace phenomenon
To be happy to observe a redpoll
Or whatever birds I happen upon
But I get bogged down with controversy
And there is no end of trouble and strife
A head full of resentments is messy
Like cutting off toes with a butcher knife
Trying to make sense is a loser's game
If I try too hard I'm certain to fail
There is always someone that I can blame
With plenty of meatheads to put in jail
Writing doggerel is a saving grace
Much better than packing a can of mace.

There are always
birds flitting by
fitting in my
brain bowl
perfectly.

Whoever said that nonsense was easy?
All sensibility is pushed aside
I try to be just a little crazy
And assert a posture that's quite cockeyed
I may be lusty and may be lazy
Neither fastidious nor dignified
When learning the rules I may be hazy
Of formalities I am horrified
I'd like to see an African daisy
As long as I'm sure it is bonafide
And I'd love to savor bouillabaisse
But green pea soup I really can't abide
I like to loiter and come in with the tide
Don't have expectations — I may backslide.

This rhyming
business is just
abysmal
fizzle and
piffle.

The absence of a girlfriend is tricky
I do appreciate conversation
My expectations aren't a bit picky
And splitting up has brought a deflation
But I'm not unhappy to be alone
Now I don't have to match her schedule
I'm not spending so much time on the phone
Twining my thoughts with hers was typical
It's true I need others to be healthy
I do want a person to bounce off of
Do I want to be controlled? Not really
I'll find another way of doing love
My home is like a Zen monastery
Where probing my thought is salutary.

Nonsensical
utterance with
Kitcat keeps the
house lively.

The wiener dog is a noble creature
He doesn't care that his legs are so short
For self-confidence he is my teacher
His comportment upon the earth is stout
Looking at him you would think that he "yips"
But instead he has a mighty dog's bark
With his barrel chest he can let 'er rip
And he also has the teeth of a shark
It's said he is a good family dog
As he begs at dinner for table scraps
With such sad eyes he starts a dialogue
But his persuasive eyes are only traps
You shouldn't give in because he'll get fat
So please don't be responsible for that.

The unselfconscious
trotting gait of
the wiener dog
bespeaks dignity.

Animals are lucky that they don't think
They don't cultivate weighty opinions
Their vision and impulses are in sync
They don't agonize over decisions
They're not wasting any time on mirrors
They couldn't care less about self-image
They don't do their own accounting figures
They're not scornful — they don't do patronage
A hippo is ugly but doesn't care
Elephants are wise but they don't worry
A deer endures losses but doesn't swear
An aging lion doesn't feel sorry
Humans are burdened with conflicting thoughts
We tie ourselves in complicated knots.

But there's poignancy
and redemption in
simplifying
burdened
thought.

Seeds of the poem are in the first line
Only a hint will make a beginning
And fibrous roots become curious twine
This open moment is worth exploring
Ideas may be lively and playful
Syllables take on rhythm and meaning
My inspiration tends to be grateful
Don't know what I am anticipating
Might I journey in any direction?
Line after line compels a commitment
I like the subtlety of inflection
Looking back I can see I'm consistent
Sincerity of purpose will evoke
An acorn creates a mighty bur oak.

I could have been
a resentful drunk —
today I cultivate
hints of
possibility.

Buds of the trees are irrepressible
Sunlight is becoming solicitous
This lively season is unquenchable
But I do feel a little wistfulness
Air in spring is quite intoxicating
I won't allow myself to be inside
Is it my heart or the sun pulsating?
Though after a while I am getting fried
As I have lived though many springs before
And each one appears a resurrection
But I am really not young anymore
And can't stop my having circumspection
The spring is always extrasensory
And I carry a weight of memory.

Apple blooms are
on the way while the
intimacy I've known
has gone away.

There is a chemistry between people
An ease of comfort or nervous tension
As our experience isn't equal
Which affects our manner of expression
There are two women of my acquaintance
With each one I behave differently
With one I exhibit loving patience
With the other verbal dexterity
Each one elicits a version of me
And with both I'm being true to myself
I am behaving spontaneously
They are also genuinely themselves
Without you I don't know who I could be
I discover you and you unfold me.

Alone with my
thoughts so much
of my thinking is
conversation
reverberating.

Rhyming is a game so don't expect much
It's not really serious but it's fun
I want to imitate a feather's touch
Before you notice the poem is done
Just being sensible can be messy
What can I do with galloping nonsense?
And can I make my proofreaders fussy?
Correcting faulty grammar can be tense
Sometimes I think that I'm wasting my time
There are productive chores to be doing
I could be putting on a pantomime
Then I wouldn't have to write anything
But rhyming and fooling can be handy
Reducing today to cotton candy.

It's tricky to make a pun
Only for a bit of fun
Ignoring my work
And going berserk
And suddenly I am done.

It's a shame that I have to be wary
That often it's better to be quiet
Politics these days has gotten scary
And it's necessary to be private
I thrive on intellectual questions
I like to parse the various issues
But want to do it without aggression
The need for honest debate continues
But I've never seen such intolerance
It's easy to be smeared as a "hater"
But it's vile a mass of incoherence
With worse consequences coming later
The media is revolutionized
Public discussions have been brutalized.

I'd like to think
friendships are immune
to political pressures
but it's better not to
test.

It is clever to make accusations
Hurling narratives of collective guilt
It's a crafty form of misdirection
As the opposition cowers and wilts
Groups of people are said to be hateful
Based on perceptions of race or gender
While the accusers themselves are spiteful
And guilty of what they say of others
Trained activists are making the charges
Accusing innocent working people
The supposed solutions are mirages
The hatred created may be lethal
It is a dirty dishonest system
Persuading people that they are victims.

Leverage comes from
accusing the innocent
and directing
an army of
angry victims.

America is in turmoil today
Even in the midst of prosperity
Our trust in each other is giving way
We don't appreciate our luxuries
And we are shredding our institutions
Cops are suspects of criminal intent
Celebrities call for prosecution
There are surging rages of discontent
Controversies are splintering our schools
Is America an evil nation?
We can't agree on societal rules
The news is full of rabid gyrations
And public discourse dispenses venom
Every news cycle is now a weapon.

Disconnecting from
the news isn't a
protection from
societal drift.

Resentment is a terrible master
Inspiring malignant obsessions
An attractive trick for news broadcasters
Spurring the viewers' latent aggressions
The news depicts the plight of victimhood
Seizing events and forming narratives
But pivotal details aren't understood
Shaping opinion is imperative
Scorn is focused on the perpetrators
Those whom the media want to destroy
Reporters assume the role of saviors
Directing hate is a lucrative ploy
Humans have an appetite for anger
It seems an unappeasable hunger.

Am I not as guilty
as those whom I
accuse? Escaping
resentment is
tricky.

Life doesn't fit in simple narratives
Choices are a maze of complexity
It's not helpful to be comparative
Much better to consider empathy
Resentment is a terrible poison
It's not worth the self-consuming fury
Even for justifiable reasons
It makes all other emotions heavy
But the pain of resentment helped me change
I had to learn the art of letting go
Mistrusting my own thoughts at first was strange
I had to cultivate a faith and grow
I suffered a measure of frustration
Enough to desire liberation.

Resenting is like
setting my own house
on fire and
refusing to
escape.

Not every thought I have is worth my time
So many are habitual nonsense
It is an exuberant game to rhyme
Which demands a little reconnaissance
And words resemble a workingman's tools
With usage comes familiarity
It does take practice to master the rules
There is play in verbal dexterity
Mastering facts is the goal of science
And I sprinkle my poems with the truth
Truth and whimsy may make an alliance
Much better than having a wisdom tooth
It is easy to get lost in my head
I'd much rather juggle with words instead.

Every day I am thinking
And my spirits are sinking
But I can waste time
Attempting to rhyme
And I will end up winking.

One is pronounced a hippopotamus
While two are termed as hippopotami
But it's different with rhinoceros
Because we do not say "rhinoceri"
Words are wiggly and they make me weary
There are many ways to spell the vowels
Thankfully we do have dictionaries
Otherwise I would very often scowl
I use the words but didn't invent them
English has become an awful mishmash
What is the logic behind the word "phlegm"?
Thinking too much will summon a whiplash
Who coined the happy word "propitious"?
It is useful for being facetious.

Words are indispensable
They make the world sensible
If I couldn't talk
I would have to squawk
Which isn't delectable.

April in Minnesota is crazy
We just enjoyed days of summery heat
With humidity that made me lazy
Followed by these days of wintery sleet
The buds are growing and the grass is green
I expect that tulips are on the way
The leaves will have an incandescent sheen
But today the sky is a mass of gray
And I am seeing snow on every roof
And my bicycle has gotten a flat
So it's not hard for me to stand aloof
At least we're not swatting at swarming gnats
Temperate weather arrives when it does
April's as crazy as it ever was.

My bicycle tire is fixed
I've ordered new tires
and a bicycle
computer for
mileage and speed.

The news is heavy with tragic events
A police shooting has happened again
Convulsing America with suspense
Because riots are happening again
People are divided by what they see
We are forming into suspicious groups
Our differing narratives don't agree
But who are justified and who are dupes?
Few can counter the tides of history
The Buddha said that the world is burning
Why tragedy comes is a mystery
We are angry and the streets are burning
The best I can do is watch and let go
Society is always full of woe.

I don't know how
liberation comes
but I'm pretty sure
not from anger.

By myself on the way to Amsterdam
I remember the White Cliffs of Dover
Taking the ferry and the trains and trams
I found a love I've not gotten over
Inside of a book of Shakespeare's sonnets
I was a lonely student at Oxford
Seeking love in solitary moments
Feeling emotions that didn't accord
I was piqued by his pitiful laments
By his lusty and cloying strategy
And by his utterly sincere pretense
With metaphorical rascality
But most of all I loved his playful words
And everything else was kind of absurd.

I admired the hearty
way Shakespeare had
of making words flow
and resonate.

Shakespeare was a superior playwright
But in sonnets he became an actor
Assuming the role of a lover's plight
Striking poses of impassioned fracture
He was in love with someone much younger
And much lamented his impending death
Implying unappeasable hunger
Dreading the expiration of his breath
He contrived to make his lover guilty
By pretending to let his lover go
Slighting himself — soliciting pity
And then he turned to braggadocio
Deploying all the tricks that words can do
Plotting to finagle a rendezvous.

While I waited for a train
in Amsterdam Shakespeare
cast a spell on me.

I could let my mind drift away with clouds
They are wispy and moving south today
They often cover the sky like a shroud
But I could let the clouds take me away
The trees are an enticing counterpoint
Without a wind they stand so peacefully
They're an infinity of crooks and joints
They are expressing themselves quietly
I love to watch the procession of light
Seeing contrails of a jetliner drift
It's easy to discount the joys of sight
And to forget that my eyes are a gift
But so much thinking goes on in my head
I get stuck in controversy instead.

I am not free of
the compulsion
to organize myself
and make decisions.

I'd rather not be guarded with my words
Because I love easy conversation
But it's true I am a bit of a nerd
And can't meet everyone's expectations
With certain people I discuss the news
But with some those topics are out of bounds
Because we have to share similar views
Otherwise there's too much trouble around
If you ask me I'll tell you what I think
And I'm sure it would be enjoyable
It is joyous to find ourselves in sync
But first I'd like you to be flexible
I don't insist that we need to agree
But I desire the grace to be carefree.

With some people
I can sense a brick wall
existing behind
their eyes.

Saturday is an oasis for me
When I sit at my desk writing poems
Being as nonsensical as I please
Typing my lines of rambunctious hokum
I had a girlfriend much smarter than me
I would visit her about once a week
But we couldn't agree ultimately
So now we're separate and we don't speak
I don't really know what happened that day
Suddenly she was unhappy with me
I expect I'll find another someday
One who's much less complicated maybe
Saturday is free — I do what I want
It's easy for me to be nonchalant.

Shakespeare made
such a big deal out of love
but I am suspicious —
was it all an act?

So much of life is indescribable
There is only so much that words can do
The forms of the trees are ineffable
Can't always explain what I think is true
The sun and the clouds are quite beautiful
But can't exactly articulate why
Consciousness is incomprehensible
I try to think but my thoughts go awry
Will I go to sleep and never wake up?
Did I come to the earth from somewhere else?
I am confused — will I ever grow up?
Is this all that there is — with nothing else?
How much am I free to think what I want?
I can relax with a buttered croissant.

A single cloud is
transforming in
the sky at a
gentle pace.

Let these pages enfold my memory
I don't want to feel the weight anymore
I don't remember very cleverly
What I recall I would rather ignore
What stands out is painful experience
All the things that I would like to forget
All the disappointed reminiscence
Let me skillfully use the alphabet
I will give my essence to these pages
Let my memory be within this book
And let the book be the one that ages
I can fashion out a witty scrapbook
I want to be smartly spontaneous
Like the sky itself — momentaneous.

The sky doesn't remember
yesterday as it's awake and
liberated.

Actors know the power of their faces
They reflect the subtlest emotions
Sincerity and empathy graces
Expressing that which remains unspoken
They say so much with a cast of their eyes
Summoning pity with tremulous lips
Utterly convincing when telling lies
It's hard to believe they're following scripts
They must embody emotions themselves
Feeling the sadness and disappointment
Adopting the aggressions that compel
With authenticity being poignant
I have to wonder who they really are
Doing what's needed to become a star.

The best actors
don't overplay
but genuinely
express what's
put on.

Do I really desire to fall in love?
Or is it best to encourage friendship?
Do I want a lover's passion? Sort of
Perhaps it's best to have companionship
But do I want the grip of obsession?
I know what it's like to become consumed
Nagging jealousy comes with possession
A desperate attachment is perfumed
Observe what love did to William Shakespeare
Love made him gesticulate like a fool
Emotions are hard — especially fear
And rejection can seem utterly cruel
So I don't know what will happen to me
And all I can do is to wait and see.

Romantic love
isn't gentle — it's
like being run over
by a Mack truck.

Kitcat is expert at rascality
But I can't say that he's a deep thinker
He likes to show off his dexterity
When evading my grasp he's a slinker
He's crafty at grabbing my attention
He'll knock containers off the kitchen counter
Then he'll look at me with expectation
Wanting to spark a nutty encounter
But I don't chase I just expostulate
I stay on the couch while waving my arms
I'm often pretending to be irate
But I'm sure that he knows I mean no harm
He's not very brainy but is a clown
Making me grateful that he is around.

While he lays on his back
we slap and swat
hands and paws
and he tries to bite
while I sing nonsense.

They often come about the size of peas
But once in a while they're elephantine
Then I am surprised and certainly pleased
So weighty with juice and tasting so fine
They're shipped to America from Chile
Which really is a modern miracle
They're not necessary — but are frilly
And they do make my breakfast magical
I combine their flavor with banana
I do love my exotic morning fruit
I sprinkle both upon my granola
They give my appetite a mighty toot
They come here — even in February
What would I do without my blueberries?

The skim milk
that completes
the ensemble is
pleasingly
bland.

When my energy wanes and peters out
My attitude is unreliable
I discover myself consumed with doubt
My ambitions are unbelievable
Then I compare my progress with others
Seeing I lack the friends that many have
That I haven't had my share of lovers
And then my battered ego needs a salve
But this has happened many times before
I know such thoughts are unreliable
So I don't debate myself anymore
And harmony is unsustainable
Energy naturally ebbs and flows
I don't punish myself when I am low.

Surfing
melancholy
is easier.

I am out of step with fashion today
Poets now are revolutionary
I don't want the outrage that they convey
Prefer to avoid verbal savagery
I do not believe in collective guilt
Quite distrust their poisonous narratives
I'd rather compose a different script
Can't be so resolutely negative
But poets are out of fashion also
No one reads poetry much anymore
Can poets make money? I don't think so
We aren't celebrated in the bookstores
Don't really care that I'm out of fashion
I write poetry for satisfaction.

I
love
to
make
the
words
dance.

Does Shakespeare comport with Japanese Zen?
Elizabethan poems are wordy
The bard wrote with honeyed metaphors then
English poetry is much more heady
The Japanese are sparing with their words
They don't invest so much in verbiage
And yet they are effective with their verbs
They slice delusion with a razor's edge
Zen is a practice based on clarity
And Japanese poetry is concise
I admire Shakespeare's dexterity
And in his wordiness he is precise
Emulating both may just be crazy
Whatever I do can't be lazy.

I adore
Matsuo
Basho's
frog jumping
into a temple
pond.

I do my best to be open to life
To forget the burdens of yesterday
To forge of myself a very keen knife
And slice through the troubles along my way
But I know I can't function on my own
That life is better when someone loves me
That people don't prosper living alone
That it is healthy for us to agree
I want to grasp hold of true perceptions
And to minimize my own disturbance
To take ownership of my selections
To be balanced in every occurrence
We are thrust on the point of becoming
And something propitious is coming.

I can't see
around corners
and can only
clarify me.

I am grateful to see hypocrisy
As it shows me clearly what not to do
Some are brazen in their mendacity
But it's sometimes hard to see as I do
Opinions vary and we don't agree
We come at things from various angles
That it's hard to know the truth — I concede
Omniscience is given to angels
There is a tinge to denunciations
A tactile hint of falsification
Making me question their accusations
They are broadcasting a mad delusion
And the hypocrites are always angry
Which sooner or later summons gangrene.

A person has to watch
for contradictory
behavior over time
to spot hypocrisy.

The sky has the virtue of emptiness
Its true quality is invisible
Its conversion is instantaneous
Always spontaneously flexible
A cloudless sky isn't really empty
The life of the sunlight is pouring down
Soliciting oxygen from the trees
The stars are visible after sundown
And winter is often shrouded with clouds
Then the earth is saturated with rain
And in summer the thunderheads resound
In every season sunlight comes again
But the sky itself is not the weather
It's the emptiness holding the weather.

The cosmos is not
galaxies and time
it is emptiness holding
galaxies and time.

In the winter I wrote about tulips
Because it's good to be optimistic
So I imagined the blooming tulips
Lifting my mood by being artistic
It's been a chilly and a dreary spring
Had I known I'd have been disappointed
I can't predict what the future will bring
It's very easy to be downhearted
But it's rainy today and I don't care
I am even quite enthusiastic
What comes today I can easily bear
I am doing spiritual gymnastics
Cavorting with words will lighten my mood
Without playing tricks my life would be skewed.

By the garage
today I see
red and yellow tulips
come up simultaneously
with daffodils.

In Washington D.C. cherry trees bloom
During the warm early days of April
But how can anyone escape the gloom
At the site of national betrayal?
In Japan they celebrate plum blossoms
That appear in February and March
They are such sweet and delicate blossoms
When beauty and the end of winter merge
And in Japan they enjoy Golden Week
Which happens within the first week of May
Everyone celebrates which is unique
As the cherry blossoms brighten their days
And also in May wisteria comes
When purple flowers exquisitely bloom.

The Japanese bestowed
the gift of cherry trees
on Washington D.C. —
the city of our
political disease.

Most of April has been damp and soggy
Puddles are collecting on my driveway
My apple trees are barren and gnarly
They don't blossom until the end of May
Giving me something to look forward to
I've mowed the lawn but it's growing slowly
And outside now I don't have much to do
At least it's unlikely to be snowy
I love my lilac bush and apple trees
When they bloom I quietly celebrate
And I welcome seeing the bumblebees
Spring comes in Minnesota — it's not late
My wiry lilac bush and apple trees
Determinedly persist through the deep freeze.

In late May the scent
of lilac and apple
blossoms mingle
over my yard
for about a week.

A downpour spattering on the concrete
Along with bamboo knocking together
Such a welcome release from sticky heat
That all these years later I remember
We were lying near the open window
Wrapped in warm blankets upon our futons
A married couple living in Kyoto
With so much youthful drama going on
It's a memory of a vanished time
Of the sensations that return to me
Of my own emotional pantomime
Remembering is important to me
There was so much life ahead of us then
I'd love to have the time over again.

Some
memories
abide
and I
don't know
why.

The alphabet is sophisticated
It gives the language organization
Sounds and meanings can be regulated
With dictionaries for definitions
Takes so much time to get educated
I've learned the grammatical conventions
A thrust of culture is indicated
A system aiding my comprehension
Eventually I've graduated
Discover myself in competition
Our society is complicated
Producing a little hypertension
I admit to my share of pretension
And I may even foster dissension.

Gazing at the
wild gesticulation
of the trees is an
antidote to
human thought.

How do you measure your velocity?
Do you enjoy an appetite for speed?
Do you have time for curiosity?
Is finishing early a worthy need?
Who could resist youthful precocity?
Is desire unambiguously greed?
What is the source of generosity?
Do you embody unknowable seeds?
Is there advantage in ferocity?
What does an obsessive ambition feed?
What is the goal of reciprocity?
Does genuine unselfish love succeed?
Is there any use in loquacity?
Or is it only harmless verbosity?

You may think you are
stationary but really
you are moving at
one thousand miles an hour
rotating upon the earth.

I admire a writer who scolded me
He was a professor but gave it up
He's intelligent and can be cranky
He loves literature with no letup
With his family he moved to Vermont
Choosing to live a simple farming life
A genuinely naïve dilettante
They struggled to survive — he and his wife
They started out as hippie homesteaders
Indulging whimsy — not experience
Now they are clever and weathered farmers
Overcoming hardships with resilience
All his life he's been writing and reading
And I find his opinions compelling.

I disparaged rhyming
and he chided me
remarking rhyming makes
remembering poetry
easier.

I sure wouldn't want to live without friends
Because easy conversation is fun
We can find things to do on the weekends
So life is joyous over the long run
But I have to watch my expectations
I need to practice giving and taking
I have to show my appreciation
Can't be the one that's always receiving
It is better to have two points of view
To have a lively and friendly debate
And maybe more or less both views are true
There's a confusing world to celebrate
To keep a friend I have to be graceful
Otherwise I could end up remorseful.

Demanding
and
expecting
is the death
of friendship.

This week I've seen a wasp and dragonflies
Today is filled with the heat of the sun
Spring is always a tonic for the eyes
Opening my windows again is fun
It's part of my life to drive around town
I watch the metamorphosis of trees
I meditate with my car windows down
I see the world parading by at ease
The leaves of trees are unfolding again
Foliage is brightly multicolored
My movement outside is carefree again
The liveliness of earth is uncovered
There comes a point with the unfolding leaves
When I rejoice with the beauty of trees.

Suddenly
effervescent
foliage dazzles
the landscape
again.

The geese and swallows and turkey vultures
The crows and eagles and the chickadees
I see them fly and they make me wonder
What would life be like to be feathery
The quality of the wind and the air
Is common to them all but each of them
Takes to their wings with a suitable flair
And they manage the blusters as they come
I see the crows get blown off of their course
I watch the geese adapt in formations
Eagles are experts at focusing force
Vultures will soar on thermal vibrations
Swallows flicker and turn like acrobats
Chickadees are delicate acrobats.

The birds are not
separate from the
air and wind and
earth and trees
and the seasons.

I believe my cellphone is wearing out
Because I have to charge it all day long
Perhaps the battery is burning out
With a replacement I could carry on
But there are faster phones on the market
With speedier internet connections
With better attractive apps to pocket
Prompting a festival of selections
Perhaps I have forgotten my passwords
Resetting them again is a hassle
Reducing me to a frustrated nerd
Lost in a technological dazzle
I like to be hypnotized by my phone
It is much more fabulous than the moon.

I would feel
practically naked
adrift and isolated
without a functioning
cellphone.

Fingers and toes — elbows knees and ankles
I flex them each day of my existence
They do so much more than merely dangle
They offer me primary assistance
I couldn't ride a bike without my knees
Couldn't have breakfast without my elbows
With ankles I can gambol at my ease
With ankles and knees I can really flow
My fingers are most handy instruments
Futzing with a cellphone and computer
For scratching they are such good implements
I can unfasten buttons as a lover
But I'm not sure what my toes are doing
Trimming toenails is excruciating.

My fingers assist
in the trimming of
toenails but I
really have to
scrunch myself.

Dandelions are appearing again
Simultaneous with creeping charlie
Asserting themselves following the rain
Dandelions are certainly hardy
I am the only one who mows my lawn
It's my weekly responsibility
For more than twenty years I've carried on
Watching dandelion fertility
I used to think of them as nasty weeds
Their presence disturbed my tranquility
I resented the puffs that spread their seeds
But I have gained some flexibility
I don't think about what I'm stepping on
Just doing what I do — mowing the lawn.

After the puffs of seeds
dissipate in spring
the persistent yellow
flowers are cheerful.

I'm learning what to do with solitude
How do I manage thinking by myself?
All my hours are filled with my attitude
How may a person be good to oneself?
For a year I've taken to watching trees
And they don't show an inch of symmetry
These are the days of the unfolding leaves
A time of natural festivity
I especially like crabapple trees
I enjoy the color of their flowers
They bloom and leaf simultaneously
I absorb their beauty and can't be sour
Feeling optimism is a power
I turn to trees almost every hour.

Even when motionless in
the absence of a wind
the trees are weirdly
expressive.

Society is divided today
With political animosity
Even during the lovely days of May
The media conveys hostility
The pandemic virus has been awful
We have shut the schools and closed businesses
A year of sickness has been terrible
Many have died but most are witnesses
We are so suspicious of each other
That our leaders are the targets of scorn
In isolation everyone suffers
So many are too furious to mourn
And yet between my friends and family
I have the grace of a community.

Some of the leaves
are almost fully
grown while others
are only budding.

I am looking forward to normalcy
When we can go to places without masks
When we can mingle again carelessly
And then I will dump my masks in the trash
Our aimed-for goal is herd immunity
Everyone needs to be vaccinated
Shots are dispersed in each community
Soon we hope to be emancipated
The New York Times has other opinions
A writer doubts our herd immunity
Too many are making bad decisions
So we will mask up indefinitely
Too many are refusing to get shots
My stomach is tied in terrible knots.

There is suspicion
that elite leadership
doesn't want to relinquish
the power of
domination.

I practice arranging thoughts into lines
Putzing in the selection of the words
Adding the ornamentation of rhymes
While admitting that the rhyming is absurd
The lines are composed of symbols and signs
Pretending to mirror reality
As if words and reality align
And the facts and my emotions agree
The left margin is making a sideline
Always anchored with capital letters
But my exuberance isn't confined
It's getting easy to burst the fetters
Every day my intentions are the same
This poetry is a light-hearted game.

The pages are composed
of numbered Houdini tricks
with words signifying
hours of frivolity.

—*Tekkan*

Book II

There is a person whom I resented
Over a question of who's dominant
Our opinions are starkly divided
And on occasion I am obstinate
We have argued at social gatherings
And afterward I considered who won
When alone I found myself arguing
The consequences of fighting weren't done
Eventually I chose to walk away
Leaving behind some people whom I like
Which has led to more solitary days
But it's better than getting into fights
And now I haven't seen him for a while
Until yesterday when he waved and smiled.

I drove ahead
with much
lingering
bitterness
dissipated.

My eyesight has always been terrible
I depend totally on my glasses
In choosing frames I am fashionable
Believing that my round frames are classics
But my lenses are chipped and breaking down
A bifocal part has become fuzzy
I went to the optometrist in town
Resigned to spend a lot of my money
And he told me about my cataracts
That it's almost time to have them removed
Afterward I won't need glasses perhaps
That my vision would be so much improved
But I'm waiting to get on Medicare
Making the expense easier to bear.

I'm used to seeing
through the smudges
And nicks of my
lenses.

Some of the leaves are almost fully grown
Other trees are only starting to bud
But is anything growing on its own?
Doesn't everything depend on a tug?
My apple trees are leafing and blooming
Without a reference to a calendar
Do they grow as they do without choosing?
Do they take their cues from the atmosphere?
I let my apple trees influence me
I planted them and have watched them growing
Through the years they are pacifying me
Apple blossom scent will soon be flowing
Apple trees and lilacs bloom together
But I don't believe that they are tethered.

It's a happy
coincidence my
lilacs on the corner
bloom with my
apple trees.

A part of me enjoys a gloomy day
When the clouds are heavy and threaten rain
When high expectations are thrust astray
Because a part of me likes to complain
I may be bad-tempered and that's OK
I am stuck at the moment and feeling strain
I can give myself a little leeway
Because elation is hard to maintain
It's good that my plans are in disarray
What is best for me I don't ascertain
I am happy to toss mistakes away
I'm just being moody — I'm not insane
I may turn my thinking without delay
Being jubilant again is child's play.

I can let the drama
drain out of my head
like air escaping
a balloon.

I waste a lot of time composing rhymes
Do you think I'm making the world better?
Poetry isn't a dreadful pastime
Cleaner than fixing a carburetor
And I try to finish before lunchtime
Afterward I work on my newsletter
No one can become a poet full time
Not without ending up as a debtor
Christopher Marlow is my paradigm
Another Elizabethan writer
But I cover the news in the meantime
I'm always looking for new subscribers
The daily news just encapsulates crime
I want a diversion from all that grime.

We have to do something
With our time —
half rhyme
eye rhyme
ragtime
pantomime.

You surely are a beautiful woman
With a delicate neck and slender shoulders
Which comport so well with ample bosoms
A striking effect on this beholder
You're posing with a careless nonchalance
Projecting unconscious self-confidence
A vision for a passion to ensconce
I savor looking without consequence
Obviously a force to contend with
A formidable conjuror of love
A risky obsession to befriend with
And once smitten so hard to dispose of
It is fetching what you do with your eyes
I don't want to believe they're telling lies.

We haven't even
spoken a word to
each other yet you've
seized my attention
with your eyes.

Do you know the word "equanimity"?
It means a person possessing balance
It is protection from fragility
Being quiet and stable is a talent
I know what it's like to be caught by love
Always desiring — living with tension
It's a trap I'm happy to be free of
It's not fun to engender suspicion
My trouble is I become possessive
Then I wonder does she really love me?
Launching thinking that becomes obsessive
I get so encumbered I can't be free
Then I start to question my dignity
My life gets tangled in perplexity.

Could I love without
engendering
possession and
suspicion?

I was given the *dharma* name "*Tekkan*"
In a ceremony involving vows
My name comes from the Zen master Dogen
His inspiration moves our Buddhist vows
He's a central figure in history
As the founder of Zen within Japan
Maybe he graces my trajectory
The name "*Tekkan*" signifies "Iron Man"
A disciple with determination
That is what my name indicates in me
I've been practicing without cessation
I do my meditation happily
But most of all I watch how I'm thinking
I aim my practice towards balanced living.

Equanimity
compassion
benevolence
altruistic joy
is the way.

Thank you — reader — for following my words
You are lending me the use of your eyes
Perhaps we are both a couple of nerds
It's a fancy game to epitomize
I would also like to borrow your heart
Maybe I could ask you to sympathize?
I turn curiosity into art
With queries and quizzes I synthesize
I'd like to explore the nature of love
Is its basic function to harmonize?
Is it also predatory? Kind of
Its primary trick is to mesmerize
To snare to burden and to tantalize
And all the while we tend to rhapsodize.

I don't want to minimize
And rather not maximize
Love is biblical
And formidable
And does tend to pulverize.

Imagine my surprise when she calls me
I was doing my work reading essays
As first she says that she's a divorcée
Which is more than a hint she wants to play
She says that her ex can be quite nasty
He expected much — she couldn't obey
Her married life was boring and messy
And she heard me speaking the other day
I seemed so intelligent and carefree
She's curious about what I have to say
She would like to get together with me
She suggested we meet and have coffee
Asking "Which are the days that I am free?"

I do distrust fantasy
I'm wary of vanity
But she is so bold
Over a threshold
Beyond rationality.

I am having trouble concentrating
The daily news has lost my interest
That phone conversation was breathtaking
And now my thinking is incoherent
I would rather not be fantasizing
I can see her tricks — I'm not ignorant
I have my essays to be editing
But I find myself a little listless
She certainly is disorienting
I could almost profess to be witless
I can see myself prevaricating
It's getting hard to focus on business
I'd like to say that this is irritating
But in my heart I know it's exciting.

She is precipitating
I am participating
Could this be love?
Coming from above?
As I am fantasizing.

She was brash to call me and I was shocked
I didn't anticipate such a move
And I was stimulated as we talked
The fact that she reached out to me is huge
She's lonely and newly separated
Desiring to know how I'm getting by
She's sad and wants to be educated
She thinks I'm cheerful and wants to know why
How is it that troubles don't get me down?
Her husband told her so many damn lies
She certain that he's been fooling around
And I'm the lucky guy who caught her eye
Suddenly my life is turned upside down
I am different but I don't know how.

I am appreciated
And now I am elated
My heart is beating
My mind is racing
I've become captivated.

This is the time of the year for lovers
The sun's bursting with energy again
So much liveliness to rediscover
And I'm feeling exuberant again
Flowering trees are at the fullest bloom
Most of the leaves are almost fully grown
Warm summer breezes are arriving soon
I may find a love that I've never known
It's so nice to be appreciated
My life has taken on a sudden turn
Which I could not have anticipated
What's coming next I really can't discern
Been a long time since I've felt so happy
I won't say more because I'll get sappy.

Now I am speculating
My heart is palpitating
And I can't sit still
As I'm feeling thrills
I am anticipating.

And now I have her number on my phone
We're meeting at Caribou for coffee
My expectations are not overblown
I intend to be a real softie
I don't remember feeling this before
A superfluity of energy
I've reached a state of opening new doors
But now my mind is wandering strangely
I'm questioning — what is she really like?
And will our conversation be easy?
I'd like to believe that we think alike
I'm getting hints that she may be teasy
She is a cutie with an easy smile
She comports herself with a sense of style.

Life is now propitious
I'm suddenly ambitious
I'm having a yen
Apart from my Zen
I'm feeling adventurous.

I am fine and I have my work to do
I have to settle and to concentrate
There are essays to edit in a queue
I need to clear my head to operate
The essays are about society
I have to correct syntax and grammar
It's important to show sobriety
Because we address serious matters
Love is very fine but now I'm busy
I just want to sit and to do my work
Can't let myself entertain a tizzy
This obsessive passion is quite a quirk
A week ago I lived differently
Considered affairs indifferently.

I like articulation
And also speculation
Want to be useful
And also truthful
I don't like agitation.

You keep me waiting and I am bemused
Waiting for you to get off of the phone
I am a little put off and confused
Standing awkwardly quietly alone
I'm sure you noticed that I have arrived
As I anxiously await our first date
Your sudden busyness does seem contrived
So what else am I to anticipate?
It seems you have a good sense of timing
You know how long to keep me suspended
Then you turn the mood by sweetly smiling
My budding frustration is upended
Part of me recognizes clever tricks
And part of me ignores — getting a kick.

I am excitedly
matched with a
voluptuous
temptress.

There's excitement in being overmatched
Encountering fresh and challenging games
Stimulated yes but not overwhelmed
I am not unskilled in using my brain
She's wispy slender and possesses grace
Getting divorced is difficult for her
She has such an innocent pixie face
There are lawyer expenses to incur
Her husband is now an alcoholic
How she asks do I live without boozing?
Living sober I say is a frolic
It's an unburdened life of my choosing
I am careful not to gaze at her breasts
Taking only glimpses I think is best.

She is genuinely
engaged and
interested in my
spiritual
practice.

She knows her husband isn't a nice guy
But he's been a very good provider
She's put up with his drinking and his lies
She's wanted to help but he's defied her
He is an electrical engineer
They had a large and luxurious house
Things have gotten ugly over the years
Until now he's no better than a louse
Their two grown sons have come to despise him
They are out of the house and on their own
They're exhausted and disgusted with him
The family cohesion has broken down
She's much happier living by herself
And he can drink all he wants by himself.

Her dad died early
of alcoholism and
her ex-husband's
an ugly drunk.

She knows people who have heard me speaking
She's heard I'm eloquent and effective
That I manage to live without drinking
That I'm compassionate and reflective
She wants to learn spiritual principles
And what sobriety is based upon
Her former life has made her cynical
Faith in religiosity is gone
I am in a peculiar position
A place beyond my anticipating
No longer burdened by inhibitions
Now I know my heart is palpitating
I've not been so flattered and exalted
Can't remember being so excited.

I'm supposed to be mindful
of equanimity
but such is not my
emerging
propensity.

Is this disembodied experience?
I'm becoming so infatuated
She's tantalizingly mysterious
She's passionate and yet understated
Daydreaming of her is luxurious
During the night my thoughts are excited
Losing sleep is creating weariness
I have a fear of being deflated
Perhaps she is just being curious
And her affections are calculated
Maybe I am driven by prurience
Are my possibilities limited?
Is both lusting and loving spurious?
My state of being is precarious.

Is it love or lust
that's intoxicating?
If there were medicine
would I take it?

Are such strong passions deleterious?
My serenity is dissipated
Complicating my Zen experience
But shouldn't loving be celebrated?
I'm finding my moods can be various
When doubting myself I'm devastated
Balancing feelings is precarious
Such crazy emotions are serrated
And then I find myself gregarious
Pondering her praise makes me elated
More than happy — I am delirious
I suspect I'm overstimulated
Now I am so oddly situated
But isn't love to be venerated?

In the lotus posture
a position of the
body I've practiced
more than thirty years
I must appear — serene.

To call or not to becomes a question
How to measure the weightiness of time
Her words and gestures — full of suggestions
I'm tending to business in the meantime
I am reading the daily narratives
The pressure of politics is extreme
Freighted with dishonest declaratives
The daily hypocrisy is routine
And how could I bring her to understand?
When it's taken me years to learn the game
The phony slogans are absorbed offhand
But the sound bites and truth are not the same
I do care about our society
And that may be a liability.

To the
uninitiated
making myself
understood
is difficult.

Having opinions is only human
We take possession without much thinking
I try to penetrate my delusions
To follow guidelines without much clinging
I begin each day with meditation
I watch thoughts come and let them dissipate
Part of me laughs at my own gyrations
I let my ideas proliferate
Love and politics are complicated
How could I not become a partisan?
I want results to be consummated
Propaganda may be bipartisan
Strong emotion is intoxicating
A lovely woman is hypnotizing.

A turkey vulture
warms his wings
circling in a
sunny thermal.

Infatuation comes in any season
And the brilliance of spring skies is lovely
Love has nothing to do with my reason
Watching my befuddlement is funny
I'm absorbed in love riding my bicycle
And propelled by the wind I'm riding swiftly
I am passionate — I am physical
And I am riding precipitously
Spring is awakening — with wide open skies
Now that swallows have returned to the fields
Their adroit maneuvers dazzle my eyes
They turn and dart and then suddenly wheel
I fly through the country over the ridge
Speed in the air on the Crossing Bridge.

Love is rippling
the vast river far below —
the sky is cloudless
and the river is cloudless
they are both shining blue.

Perhaps I'm being a bit of a clown
Being overly infatuated
And I'm afraid of being let down
I know what it's like to be deflated
My juices are flowing — capturing me
Something I hadn't anticipated
My obsession with her won't let me be
Nothing I'm doing is calculated
Thank God I'm not a judge or a lawyer
My rationality is compromised
I'll operate more cleverly later
Perhaps I'm being manipulated
Is she — or am I — doing this to me?
Is this a heaven? Or catastrophe?

My dear — you should see
me poised within the lotus
posture appearing
serenely composed within
such passionate vibrations.

Why would someone choose a nasty husband?
She did say that he's a good provider
She is clever and doesn't get flustered
She may be attracted to aggressors
And then why is she attracted to me?
She is intelligent and so am I
She wants to learn something from me maybe
And so I wonder what that signifies
I'm all about being poised and open
She knows that I'm seeking liberation
Some of us hit bottom and are broken
There's a saving grace in desperation
To do meditation isn't easy
This girl is coquettish and she's teasy.

A part of me knows
that I want to be needed
to be desired
by the opposite sex and
now I'm hungering again.

There's a paradox in liberation
At least of the type that I am seeking
Trying too hard creates separation
I'd like to give up the habit of grasping
There is the initial desperation
A lingering period of suffering
That's enough to inspire frustration
That culminates in a new beginning
From there what's needed is relaxation
A peace apart from unending striving
Fascination with subtle vibrations
There is patience to be cultivating
I want to surf with my motivations
I would like to balance with emanations.

Romantic love and
political victory
may be delusions
to be grasped only for a
moment before they dissolve.

A violin is tuned exquisitely
And then the music is quite eloquent
I don't put much faith in passivity
Believing right effort is relevant
I'd like to act with sensitivity
So is playing politics negligent?
It should be done with selectivity
My motives need to be benevolent
But can I keep my objectivity?
Or could I myself be malevolent?
There's confusion in relativity
Opponents are commonly arrogant
I need my strength and flexibility
I'd like to keep a sense of etiquette
But being passive is a detriment.

There could be peace in
doing my best and leaving
the results up to
cosmic vibrations beyond
anyone's permanent grasp.

The birds are noisy before the sunrise
Just listening is intoxicating
Their joyful persistence does hypnotize
But in truth the males are advertising
They are using voices to lionize
Each of the males is fiercely competing
When conniving for mates they dramatize
The allure of females must be enticing
Is my loving a lusting in disguise?
Even so is that disqualifying?
Are my motives getting crosswise?
Don't want to stop my anticipating
And I don't want to overanalyze
My newfound romance is energizing.

It's necessary
for a mommy and daddy
buddha to combine
before a baby buddha
can properly manifest.

A good part of me is leery of love
I don't want to be intoxicated
An obsession is hard to get rid of
Sooner or later I'll be deflated
I can go to the park and watch the sky
I will slow my mind and listen to birds
In the distance I can see a crane fly
And I'm not wasting any time on words
The birds will come and then the birds will go
The clouds and sun are constantly moving
The breeze in the trees does ebb and flow
The rabbits and the squirrels are scampering
My adoration becomes a plaything
I'm not hearing or seeing anything.

My obsession with
her overlays the breeze
in the trees — and the
crane flying — I don't see when
the crane is disappearing.

I haven't lived so long without seeing
That people get crazy involved in love
It's quite common to be fantasying
Of fitting together like hand in glove
But there is a certain reality
That one partner will become dominant
That one possesses the lock and the key
When the passion becomes less prominent
There has to be compatibility
And a forgoing of competition
There's hard work in responsibility
We would need a worthy compensation
When the romantic feeling drains away
We would live with each other every day.

It takes a while for
a real person to emerge
out from under the
fantasy and then how would
reality manifest?

The breeze in the leaves is inspiring
As the clouds are sometimes dimming the light
Simple observation is reviving
The clouds have dispersed and the sky is bright
I'm not really unhappy on my own
What I do with my time I can decide
I'm not going to be using my phone
I'm going to let this relationship slide
The vibrant sky is glorious today
I am watching as the birds come and go
I am happy this Memorial Day
No one is working and I can go slow
I can play with words and think as I please
And I don't have to let myself be teased.

I don't even know
whether her interest in me
goes beyond idle
curiosity and is
only a passing fancy.

The early sonneteers wrote about love
I've followed tradition and played my part
Is my emotion genuine? Sort of
But over the years I've guarded my heart
Love is worthy — love is necessary
Without loving we wouldn't populate
But I wonder what is best for Barry
Love takes more push than I can generate
This afternoon I'll ride my bicycle
The weather is going to be glorious
Looking forward makes me excitable
Pedaling freely is luxurious
For several days I've played Romeo
But my part was only a cameo.

The peonies are
budding with their glorious
superfluity
of lushness as their heavy
blossoms are bending their stems.

You do know how to take me by surprise
To call me in the middle of the day
You know that you're a delight for my eyes
To dangle yourself so that I obey
I had thought it better to let you go
I don't want the bother of obsession
And I am hesitant — but even so
A part of me longs to take possession
To be the body that takes your body
Of this I'm sure that you're well aware of
With all the passion that I embody
You're coaxing it forth and hinting at love
You are an unscrupulous seductress
Seizing my attention with directness.

You know enough of
my schedule to take the
opportunity
to catch me off my guard and
dazzle me with inducements.

I know you're playing on my sympathy
Praising my receptive intelligence
Relying on my ready empathy
You're expressing yourself with eloquence
You would like me to come and meet with you
You want to know how I live so simply
Won't I come to appraise what we could do?
You are confused and feeling dreadfully
How does one learn to let go of trouble?
You would like me to instruct you — you say
I can see that you're brash and quite subtle
I'd really like to come to you today
But I have chores that I have got to do
So much rigmarole to muddle through.

I know instantly
correcting and editing
syntax and grammar
hunting for hidden typos
will now be more difficult.

You want to know how not to be angry
To rise above your ex's pettiness
To not be fuming — to not be cranky
To escape the feeling of emptiness
Your daddy died of alcoholism
Your ex is a terrible drinker too
Both had narcissistic egoism
Which you ignored but really knew was true
You work during the day as a waitress
You're a happy conversationalist
And people are clueless of your distress
But the urge to chatter you can't resist
Men at work are always hitting on you
They press their luck to see what they can do.

Both your ex and your
daddy used intelligence
to be successful
providing opulent homes
in sumptuous neighborhoods.

There is some cruelty in your husband
He is disparaging and calls you names
Which is what you can no longer withstand
In response you do exactly the same
To be cutting in your comments offhand
It's easy to be critical and blame
Usually to gain the upper hand
It becomes a habit that's hard to tame
In divorce you are advancing demands
And now it's a nasty lawyering game
The goal is to gain a judge's command
There is property to righteously claim
For marriage to end like this is a shame
You are resisting an impulse to maim.

He can keep the house
in the swanky neighborhood
but he's got to sell
the boat and pay every month
a hefty spousal support.

There's more drama here than I am used to
My divorce went without complexity
Such bitterness we didn't resort to
I don't see my ex as an enemy
I guess such wild passion becomes a stew
And perhaps it's mixed up with jealousy
With so much history to muddle through
With battles continuing endlessly
And what on earth am I supposed to do
With emotion expressed desperately?
And what trouble am I getting into?
He is arrogant — she is comely
She is beautiful and he has money
He is dogmatic and she is plucky.

Were they made for each other?
To battle with one another?
To squabble and fight
Trading words that bite
Passionately together?

Not getting angry isn't so easy
I had to give up my way of thinking
To let go of victim mentality
And to stop my alcoholic drinking
You can't make a change temporarily
How does one do it without backsliding?
I had to be crushed fundamentally
Such experience isn't appealing
Hitting bottom is a necessity
Otherwise any progress is fleeting
Now I practice in a community
Communication is empowering
I need new power to grow into
A power to give my frustrations to.

The practice becomes
"Let go or be dragged."

Apparently there are some painful pleasures
Where couples come to trouble each other
Subjecting themselves to endless pressure
Jealously squabbling with one another
I wonder what she is seeing in me
Attending and speaking so carefully
Carelessly placing her hand on my knee
Moving in closely quite casually
I know what's happening — I really do
As I notice her eyes are powder blue
Such an intoxicating point of view
I will see what she wants and muddle through
Her fetching presence is tantalizing
Her voice and her words are hypnotizing.

Her curves are tantalizing
Her voice is hypnotizing
But I am careful
And I'm respectful
While she is appetizing.

You know I'm captivated by your charms
And that being with you makes me happy
How could conversing come to any harm?
We are both so fluent and word-savvy
It's not necessary to squabble and fight
I have learned how to live quite peacefully
I don't have trouble sleeping overnight
I've avoided worry successfully
The tricks of detachment I can show you
How to absorb the sunlight — how to breathe
The peace of the *dharma* I can give you
I could navigate with you if you please
You could let go of all your agitation
We could enlighten your cogitation.

Your ex knows how to
manipulate to coerce
you and to push your
buttons befuddling and
destroying your happiness.

The mind operates precariously
What we think about we give power to
Our thoughts happen so precipitously
What we think about we give ourselves to
I have governed myself deceitfully
Supposing I'm controlling what I do
Passion with peace exists uneasily
Sometimes my emotions are torn in two
I aspire to live and love gracefully
And you are showing me that you do too
To think and behave harmoniously
I'm happy to get together with you
To express and to listen equally
I've not had satisfaction recently.

I'm wondering how
such a lovely woman as
yourself could be so
taken in with a person
so unsuited to yourself?

"I was captured by his virility" —
She says — "by his aggression and his looks
His professional capability
Though I knew he was a bit of a crook
But now his behavior has gotten worse
Becoming no more than a drunken louse
There's a quality to him that's perverse
He'd rather have me shut inside the house
I see you operate differently
That you're authentically compassionate
Which is kind of rare — incidentally
And that your words are strangely resonant
I am coming to see that intelligence
Expresses an attractive elegance.

"I don't think you know
the influence of your words
I am curious
how it is you became so
intuitive?" she asks me.

I'm walking about in a happy daze
So satisfied and anticipating
My daydreaming has been a little crazed
Experience is intoxicating
And my meditation is going well
Sitting not moving for forty minutes
Absolutely no problem sitting still
I practice to keep cerebral fitness
I'm doing my editing well enough
Sometimes I am losing my train of thought
Philosophical stuff is kind of tough
Doing the business is an afterthought
In truth I'm reliving my night with her
Ordinary activities are blurred.

I am a nerd who
astonishingly caught a
delightful fish and
now the world is appearing
surprisingly different.

I'm really confused and somewhat put off
So why isn't she answering my calls?
It appears suddenly she's cut me off
Didn't expect to encounter a wall
I do remember reminding myself
Intoxication ends in depression
My sad situation speaks for itself
I guess I'm not done with learning lessons
I've got to decide what I'm going to do
I imagine myself being resolute
Maybe I did something — made a miscue?
Can't stop thinking about her attributes
I'm not going to fret — I'm not going to call
I'm not going to do anything at all.

The Chinese poet
Cold Mountain left the city
kicked off the red dirt
of civilization and
lived with mountains and rivers.

My thoughts are whirling in captivity
I can't help wondering what you're doing
I feel the lure of compulsivity
As my mind is busy speculating
I am confused within uncertainty
Weighing each of our words — analyzing
Do you control me surreptitiously?
Your motivations are mystifying
I did enjoy you unabashedly
Now your sudden absence is perplexing
What's with this unavailability?
My ignorance is disorienting
Don't know why you're not returning my calls
Suddenly you've erected a brick wall.

My ignorance and
confusion manifests in
scenarios on
top of scenarios that
only inspire longing.

You are a shadow companion to me
Everywhere I go I'm thinking of you
We had such an engaging repartee
Not many women banter as you do
Your words your beauty come along with me
You're an added dimension in my head
I've become a Romeo wannabe
I did have a hint of trouble ahead
I think I'm in love with being in love
I'm using you to hypnotize myself
It's the idea of loving I love
I'm pulling a mighty trick on myself
I'm stuck right now and don't know what to do
My head is busy imagining you.

Infatuation
is a gas transporting me
into whimsical
departures destinations
of happy permutations.

I don't have to be encumbered with you
Comport yourself exactly as you please
You are much more controlling than I knew
You are a voluptuous tricky tease
I am going to go about my business
I have many important things to do
Love is disorienting dizziness
There's more to do than to think about you
I do have my bicycle and my cat
And I can look at my cottonwood tree
You are no more trouble than summer gnats
You are not getting me to bend a knee
Our meeting wasn't serendipity
You've only taken my serenity.

I do want liberation
I enjoyed our flirtation
I not going to fret
Do you want to bet?
I don't want a fixation.

The sun has been burning so brilliantly
The roots of the growing grass are busy
There's no reason to mope despondently
To befuddle myself and become lazy
I just bought a bicycle computer
I can track my time and average speed
To discipline myself and go faster
It takes method and practice to succeed
Where you are doesn't matter much to me
I've got plenty to occupy my time
And what you're doing doesn't concern me
I think maybe I will compose some rhymes
I'm perfectly free to do as I please
Why should I bother with ticks gnats and fleas?

The world is still rotating
The hardy grass is growing
There are things to do
And places to go
There's no need to be moping.

You won't return my calls — I don't know why
I don't think I can do anything more
Probably it's better to say goodbye
It is beyond me to open your door
From now on I know what has to be done
I need to upend and guard my thinking
The excitement I felt can't be undone
You are even disturbing my sleeping
I have to stop when thinking about you
And instantly think about something else
I've got to come up with tricks that will do
I want to think about anything else
Perhaps I can tinker with poetry
And turn my attention to clarity.

Words are always enticing
Composing is inviting
I don't have to lie
I look at the sky
Dragonflies are beguiling.

My roses bloom when summer arrives
Sunny mornings in June are often cool
When the sun and the roses harmonize
That the roses don't last long is the rule
Year after year my rosebushes blossom
They are mostly white with a tinge of pink
That the sky is cloudless happens often
The mild weather and roses are in sync
I do forget the rose's sweet perfume
I have to be close and inhale deeply
The scent is a cynosure of the bloom
It's the rule that roses appear briefly
Each single blossom is ephemeral
The joy of beauty is perennial.

When clouds are absent
when mornings are often cool
the sky is filled with
immeasurable sunlight
that just happens to be blue.

A week before I didn't know my speed
I was just estimating my mileage
Without a grasp of my average speed
I couldn't make use of such knowledge
But as soon as I go fast I can tell
Whether I am doing the same — or better
Now I know what I'm doing very well
Thanks to my new bicycle computer
This little gadget on my handlebars
Is changing my ideas of biking
I know exactly how fast and how far
I'm going and whether I'm improving
But the wind is a pivotal player
An unpredictable force of nature.

Now I'm a greyhound
measuring the minutes and
the distance from
one landmark to the next
from one day to another.

Of all the things going on in a day
Some things are worthy of celebration
Even if I'm having an awful day
Some elements are worth recognition
I don't come to writing casually
I'd like to see what's going to effervesce
And to leverage curiosity
So perceptions and words may coalesce
I give myself to what I attend to
Writing focuses my sincerity
It adds significance to what I do
One of the benefits is clarity
I'd like to be as light as a feather
But tough enough for all kinds of weather.

Crossing boundaries
of what happens and how I
respond I would like
to dissolve who I think I
am and be spontaneous.

Imagine being a fish in summer
Acclimated to persisting current
Would you be sensitive to bright colors?
How often would you resist the current?
Would you be aware of what water is?
Or have an idea of the river?
Would the surface be a strange kind of fizz?
Would other fish be flashes of silver?
Would you know that the river is narrow?
What would you think of the river's surface?
Would you happily wiggle your torso?
Would you recognize your tail's service?
How much of a change would come in winter?
Would you ever have to deal with splinters?

Imagine the shock
of the sudden grasp of an
eagle's sharp talons —
the wrenching departure
from a comfy dimension.

Do you think the trees remember last year?
Does the sky have a hint of memory?
Somehow all of the elements cohere
Life is woven together cleverly
We're growing on a mysterious sphere
This moment goes on interminably
Some of my memories are very dear
But over time they become fantasy
What I'm remembering is a veneer
Memory continues tediously
My eyes and nose and tongue and skin and ears
Are open to life continuously
Experience sometimes becomes severe
I hope I can manage to be sincere.

Am I choosing to
recall as I do or is
remembering a
happening continuing
itself — independently?

When riding my bicycle I am free
I am not compelled to be productive
There are the birds and dragonflies to see
The bright panorama is seductive
The wind's a potent force of contention
The more that I push the more it resists
But even so I do find my traction
Finding a suitable pace — I persist
I don't have to go fast — but I like to
No one is compelling my exhaustion
I expend myself because I want to
With a healthy urge for satisfaction
There's a purity of strength in motion
That balances disturbing emotion.

I tend to measure
my speed against the other
riders that I come
across in a curious
urge of compulsivity.

I don't want the need to feel important
Because then I am measuring myself
And I am seeking others' endorsements
And will be busy promoting myself
Also I have a yearning to be loved
To be comprehensively understood
To comport with someone like hand in glove
Savoring companionship would be good
I am wondering from where does love come?
I think love already resides in me
But my capacity is kind of numb
With too much disturbance to set it free
Love is always there waiting for income
I have to be ready to let it outcome.

Perhaps love is
a dexterous hand
ready to engage with
the earth and people
and I am the glove.

Books can be stuck describing what happened
It need not be necessarily so
I imagine a book without an end
That captures the present and helps it grow
Because miracles are happening now
The seasons repeat again and again
Life gets increasingly burdened somehow
Surprising disappointments are a drain
But there's no ending to this moment now
I can't comprehend all that's happening
It's all simultaneous anyhow
I'm trying to get good at balancing
Can I affix words to liberation?
Don't know — but it is my aspiration.

This moment goes
on and on and all
that goes along with it
is incomprehensible
until now.

Morning is drenched in the summer sunlight
Only a few clouds are drifting southward
The whole expansive river is alight
I'm trying to capture its life with words
The heat of the sun envelops my skin
A million leaves are reflecting the light
And the clouds and the river are akin
Gentle motion is concealing their might
How can one capture this moment now?
It is the point of creativity
Numberless species are living somehow
Emerging beings in activity
There's too much going on to pigeonhole
My viewpoint is only a buttonhole.

In this happenstance
moment the river and the
wisps of the clouds are
progressing gradually
majestically southward.

I'm not going to think about her — not now
Yes — she is beautifully intelligent
I can't get ahold of her anyhow
And I'm wary of her temperament
I'm not naïve with people anymore
The way she hooked me was remarkable
With no explanation she closed the door
And she has made herself unreachable
It's not good to dwell on her lovely eyes
So piercingly intent and powder blue
I really don't think that she told me lies
After all there is nothing I can do
If I let myself go — then I'm to blame
I'm not going to be a moth drawn to flame.

Certainly she has
a most bodacious body
with such fetching curves
but I'm beyond those baubles
with important things to do.

A girlfriend would be inconvenient
I would have to live so differently
Of course there would be our disagreements
When I'd rather act independently
We would be spending evenings on the phone
Going over what happened every day
I'd have to develop a firm backbone
To get at least a portion of my way
And I would have to rearrange my house
She would be over here some of the time
It would almost be like having a spouse
Which would be bodacious part of the time
If only desire could be controlled
But it can't — it just multiplies eightfold.

I'm safely ensconced
in my abode with only
the solicitous
attention of my rowdy
male cat for entertainment.

Sometimes I wake before I intend to
And I'm lying in bed ruminating
I'd like to sleep but I'm unable to
While my head is busy cogitating
Then I'm vulnerable and defenseless
I don't have thinking — the thinking has me
I'm exhausted but my mind is restless
I'm not present — I'm stuck in memory
My life appears as a hall of mirrors
Each reflection is grossly distorted
I am masculine and I don't shed tears
I keep my emotions closely guarded
Relaxation is a wonderful gift
Learning to relax is a handy trick.

I can adopt the
lotus posture before dawn
straightening my back
folding legs over under
breathing and quieting.

It's been so dry that the grass quit growing
With only occasional scraps of clouds
Mostly from the south the wind's been blowing
And blowing on the hills the wind is loud
I wouldn't notice if I weren't riding
The pressure of wind is manageable
Maneuvering in wind is like dancing
Finding the perfect pace is possible
There's joy in motion on my bicycle
There's nothing between me and everything
Perceptions are vibrantly physical
Rushing inside the wind is exciting
I push myself approaching exhaustion
I relax achieving satisfaction.

When the wind pushes
me from behind the air is
quiet and I move
precipitously until
I turn and face its roaring.

The lift part of the bridge is in motion
And pedestrians wait at a closed gate
We riders too wait in position
The gate releases — I become the bait
Going first I leave him following me
Gliding smoothly through the crowd of people
Starting in the right climbing gear is key
I rise and dance lightly on my pedals
I've raced up this hill many times before
But usually I ascend alone
Climbing this hill is what I'm training for
I've made the slope a competitive zone
Near the top I shift to a faster gear
I don't suppose he is anywhere near.

Turning a corner
I glance behind to check for
him seeing him a
little ways behind as I
shift again increasing speed.

You surprised me again by coming here
Walking into my office with coffee
I've not thought about you — you disappeared
I did not forget about your body
You didn't bring the cups — you brought the pot
You are not a person to go halfway
When you do drink coffee you drink a lot
Doing a kind of coffee pot sashay
You're typically brash unconsciously cute
It appears that you've just got out of bed
Your breasts are looking like bulging grapefruits
For me not to see I'd have to be dead
It takes me a while to know what to say
This doesn't happen every other day.

I'm discombobulated
And inarticulated
My tongue is too slow
So my words don't flow
But I'm also elated.

You have certainly come animated
All you can do is to talk about Bruce
Just what I would have anticipated
Your soon-to-be ex is a complete louse
I say it's not worth getting agitated
And I'd like to talk about anything else
Now the way forward is indicated
He can sell the damn boat and keep the house
The divorce decree will be stipulated
You won't have to live with a drunken spouse
Aren't you happy to be liberated?
You're lucky to have gotten a townhouse
At least now I know where you're located
I don't understand why you're frustrated.

Put up with the frustration
Just do the mediation
Let the lawyers work
Don't go so berserk
You'll get your compensation.

I don't mind you coming into my life
Bursting suddenly into my office
I am not beholden to my ex-wife
And I don't want to appear standoffish
But I have questions — what happened to you?
And why did you stop returning my calls?
I wanted to talk but what could I do?
For some reason I encountered a wall
I don't know about your soon-to-be ex
From what you say he's not a nice person
It seems he has a scornful intellect
Your relationship now is going to worsen
I must say that I don't care about him
And the chances of Bruce changing are slim.

So what if he wants the boat?
Who cares if it even floats?
He may be swimming
With other women
But who cares if he's a goat?

It's just that I've been conflicted — she says —
My mind's been racing and I've been upset
And I get entangled in what he does
I have been lost in a crabby mindset
And I am not even charging my phone
I'm sorry that I've caused you to worry
But I'm spending most of my time alone
Please — could you find a way to forgive me?
I've missed your company and your kind words
Of all my friends — you — best — understand me
I've been so angry and also quite bored
I believe that you know how to help me
So — Barry — I don't know what I would do
Without a compassionate man like you.

I've had to move all my stuff
And every day has been rough
I have been weary
And also teary
I've already had enough.

She's given me a lot to think about
Can she truly not be charging her phone?
Divorce does make sensitive people pout
And I'm relieved that she says she's alone
Of all her friends I best understand her
And she chose to burst in on me today
I know the trials of divorce are severe
Few of us can really expect fair play
I don't like being left in the dark
I'm happy to be in contact again
We didn't say any unkind remarks
And perhaps both of us are under strain
I do suspect she knows what she's doing
I will not put up with any lying.

Before I had no answers
And couldn't make advances
I was damn lonely
My days were stony
I didn't like my chances.

I do like to talk to you everyday
And it's easy to be in touch by phone
It's important for me to have my say
As I think about you when I'm alone
As soon as I'm awake I love to call
And now you're answering every morning
It was hard for me when you put up your wall
But now I'm excited that we're talking
At 5 a.m. I'm calling your number
While lying in bed I'm talking to you
Our conversation allays my hunger
I yearn to talk and it seems you do too
Every morning we're having pillow talk
Sometimes I wake early and watch the clock.

Your idea to
talk on the phone at 5
a.m. before dawn
is a wonderful way to
start my day — thinking of you.

So with new habits I have to adapt
I am delaying my meditation
And rejiggering my schedule in fact
Causing more than a little disruption
I love to be able to interact
Stimulated by our conversation
Your voice is having a touching impact
Feeding an urge for anticipation
I am soaking up your daily doings
Getting to know your intimate habits
Becoming familiar with your thinking
Appreciating your verbal talents
And after our predawn conversation
I am digesting new information.

Pillow talk
predawn intimacy
is becoming the
cynosure
of my days.

You don't trust Bruce and he owes you money
You still share an account at Bremer Bank
There's a circumstance that's kind of funny
An opportunity to play a prank
He has been on a list for twenty years
To be a member of the country club
Now his number is up — his way is clear
He has $4,000 to pay up
He thinks that he can be a golfing fool
All he has to do is to pay the fee
He's clearly forgotten you know the rules
And you intend to withdraw that money
When he writes a check he will be surprised
His cherished wish will have to be revised.

The mediators
haven't decided on the
dispursal of funds
so he's not entitled to
claim his golfing membership.

Your Daddy was a smart entrepreneur
And he once owned a lumber company
And he was a successful inventor
With a patent earning lots of money
He wasn't a very faithful husband
And put your mother through enormous grief
He's reminding me of your ex-husband
There's a pattern here — that is my belief
Your Daddy drank a lot of alcohol
Normal behavior in your family
He would go to bars and get into brawls
And he died before the age of fifty
Your family did enjoy prosperity
Then suddenly you lived in poverty.

It's astounding how
drinking's a thread woven
through generations
of your family — also
affecting your brother's life.

You remember a good friend from childhood
You were swimming together at the beach
She wore a tight bathing suit with a hood
The fabric was so very tightly stretched
She was protruding and looking silly
And you couldn't stop yourself from laughing
She had chubby cheeks and a big belly
It was obvious you hurt her feelings
And you do remember feeling guilty
But the damage had already been done
You wavered between laughter and pity
While your outburst kind of ruined the fun
There's so much trauma — even from grade school
Kids can be unintentionally cruel.

You told your Dad the
story afterward because
you did feel guilty
but in the telling the two
of you couldn't stop laughing.

Your family was happy for a while
Until about your junior high school age
Your Dad dying suddenly was a trial
Your Mom struggled to make a living wage
She was forced to work a couple of jobs
There was persisting insecurity
But she did persevere against the odds
Hardship brought you early maturity
Difficulty marred your adolescence
The loss of your Daddy was a burden
He was such a dominating person
You missed his calming masculine presence
Losing your Dad was a calamity
But your Mom came through for the family.

Your Dad was a rogue
dynamically exciting
and afterward the
quiet absence in the house
was difficult to endure.

In high school you were a popular girl
You dated the football quarterback star
Those years went by in an ecstatic whirl
And I believe they made you who you are
Truthfully you didn't care about him
Your personalities didn't quite fit
He was more often suited to the gym
After graduation you knew you'd split
But you liked getting so much attention
You were talkative — you were sociable
Faux celebrity was your dimension
All this information is notable
I understand your personality
How you formulate rationality.

To me you appear
as a queen of beauty a
little worse for wear
with the slightest tinge of
dissipation about you.

After high school you attended college
At the university in Duluth
You enjoyed learning and gaining knowledge
You met Bruce and comprehended the truth
You understood his cast of character
He was a rogue and a heavy drinker
You guessed that he'd be a good provider
With him you found genuine desire
With him you had what we call chemistry
Your personalities bonded with glue
And should we say that's serendipity?
In the end it didn't work out for you
He makes a sport of disparaging you
He isn't nice — as you already knew.

Sometimes it's a shame
that like attracts like and with
time the qualities
bringing couples together
may end up destroying them.

You left college without graduating
You married and he finished his degree
His job is financially rewarding
And you started having a family
He does electrical engineering
He returned to get a master's degree
Enabling him to begin managing
Which earns an even higher salary
For him you gave up your education
Which now has become a major regret
Being limited is a frustration
Being unsupported is quite a threat
You take so much pride in both of your sons
Raising them is the best thing you've done.

You are counting on
a substantial amount of
spousal support from
the divorce decree which is
entirely justified.

You went to work when your kids entered school
And you really do enjoy waitressing
His disapproval is certainly cruel
Your freedom is beyond his controlling
You have always loved being sociable
And you are being paid to talk all day
Conversing is more than comfortable
Bantering with customers is child's play
You're getting the attention you desire
You have many relationships at work
You've transformed yourself into a server
Having wide social contact is a perk
It irks him that you are cute and friendly
That so many are complimentary.

There is a guy who
every year is buying you
a Christmas tree as
a kind of a fetish which does
tend to make Bruce unhappy.

I have never known such intimacy
My ex and I weren't nearly as fluent
I'm learning details with intricacy
I do not believe this is imprudent
Who would have believed that at 5 a.m.
I'd be talking to a lovely woman?
I'm surprised at how elated I am
I think I'm becoming fully human
New experience is blooming for me
Digesting the world through another's eyes
Conversation is good — and we agree
And communication is best without lies
Every day when I'm getting out of bed
Thoughts of her are occupying my head.

For the rest of the
day I'll be considering
new information
and how differently life
appears from another view.

I had a friend in Hutchinson Kansas
It was my first taste of companionship
With him I knew an easy happiness
I remember our genuine friendship
And fifty years on I don't recall much
But I'm aware of a hole in my heart
So much of my life I've felt out of touch
I am familiar with living apart
It's not been easy to communicate
I've put it down to mismatched chemistry
With people I tend to reach a stalemate
I live with a dose of perplexity
For easy companionship it's a must
For intimacy I have to have trust.

My family moved
from Hutchinson Kansas
to Minnesota
where in Bayport the kids
were nasty and combative.

Playing with words comes easily to me
I like to express what I'm perceiving
When saying what I want I do feel free
Clarifying my thoughts is exciting
With most people there is hesitancy
There are hidden barriers in the way
I've come to keep my distance guardedly
And too often I don't know what to say
Pristine sheets of paper open to me
I can express exactly what I want
The receptive paper and I agree
I've found a reliable confidant
There is a purity in playing with words
And I don't care if I'm sounding absurd.

The presence of the
paper serves as the best of
friends until it may
happen that a flesh and blood
person comes along I hope.

For some reason we can articulate
Conversation comes without an effort
She bandies her phrases and innovates
Our manner of relating does comport
She tells her story and it resonates
She's in a distressing situation
And for her — isolation suffocates
It's better to express the frustration
Perhaps some solutions may percolate
I'm not going to tell her what she should do
While talking — ideas may germinate
And she may grasp what she already knew
Listening carefully can be a game
I really do believe she feels the same.

If she hadn't called
me there was no way that I
would have taken the
initiative to call her —
she is uninhibited.

She understands how attractive she is
I'm astounded that she's talking to me
I know how intoxicating she is
And comprehend that there's no guarantee
I'm weighing implications in her words
Speculating what she feels about me
Nothing she is saying goes unexplored
I feel the sting of insecurity
I want to be cared about — to be loved
With her is that a possibility?
Presently the question is unresolved
The truth will emerge eventually
She is bursting with sexuality
Topping pleasing compatibility.

I don't like being
exposed but I'm already
hooked and excited
so I'm going to keep talking
and see what eventuates.

Suppose you imagine how life could be
Without the burden of inhibitions
From my point of view you're already free
You are able to change your conditions
Which you are doing by talking to me
Not being bound by self-definitions
But don't always expect to be carefree
Don't waste energy in competition
Problems with solutions tend to agree
You're not liking your present position
So envision where you would like to be
Which could be an open proposition
Perhaps judgment day for a divorcee
May well turn out to be a jubilee.

Why drag around
all those old arguments and
bitter memories
when you could be learning the
best lesson — how to relax?

Most of my anguish comes from my thinking
I don't notice what it's doing to me
I'm not supple — I'm only reacting
I would like to use spontaneity
It's a matter of developing poise
Relaxing is a propitious game
Reducing my troubles to background noise
I don't have to struggle argue and blame
So how may I relax when I want to?
Relaxing is a trick that takes practice
Of releasing thinking when I need to
My thoughts are like a prickly cactus
I accept that I may not get my way
I'll do something else on another day.

I rely on a
simple idea of a
power greater than
myself that I partner with —
this power takes care of me.

Relaxing is the hardest trick there is
Because I don't think about doing it
I concentrate on doing my business
Without a success I don't want to quit
But my relationships don't work like that
Especially when involving affections
I'm not good at manipulating that
Compelling people in my direction
I cannot make people care about me
Perhaps lovers grow into each other
I have to relax and to let things be
Somehow companions find one another
Being cheerful is very attractive
It has to be true to be effective.

I practice being
lonely and cheerful at the
same time trusting
wonderful developments
are just around the corner.

Something about me tickles your fancy
We've been conversing now every morning
I'm liking our talk — it makes me happy
Starting the day with you is exciting
We're saying hello right at 5 a.m.
There are always new topics to explore
I don't want to be hungry — but I am
I'm surprised that you're eager — but you are
The hours we're talking are filling my day
They make me ponder for deeper meanings
Afterward I consider what you say
I'm looking to foster new beginnings
Conversing on the phone every morning
Every evening is worth the waiting.

To hear your voice say
my name at 5 a.m. when
most people are still
sleeping has a certain thrill
worth the anticipation.

All relationships are perishable
I think this is something you understand
Not only if you're incompatible
Even with your sincerity on hand
Over time people grow differently
And they come to grate against each other
We all have quirks of personality
So it's good to forgive one another
But relationships don't have to perish
Can you give your partner a gentle touch?
And refrain from imposing your answers?
But who am I to talk so overmuch?
These are questions that I haven't mastered
There is something that's beyond chemistry
A loving patience is a remedy.

Maybe I'm a great
fool to be talking like this
as I'm divorced too
and spending my holidays
as a singularity.

You're angry at the cook for what he said
He accused you of being "such a woman"
It certainly seems that he's a blockhead
You could have said he's a troglodyte man
There's a lot going on at your café
Your friend Sherry is a likeable girl
She can make a new boyfriend every day
From your description she's like a showgirl
No wonder Bruce got so jealous of you
You're enjoying a vibrant social life
And I really have to give you your due
You're more than an ordinary housewife
I do like using the word "cynosure"
I think you possess plenty of allure.

Meanwhile I am all
by my lonely self at the
office going through
essays correcting grammar
redoing faulty syntax.

How lucky we were to find each other
It's so simple to have conversation
To listen and talk to one another
While cultivating our relaxation
I'm curious how your days are going
I'm giving you my eager attention
The littlest details are engaging
Enlivening our daily narration
And I also get to talk about me
And to express all of my hidden thoughts
You're giving me the opportunity
I'm getting to untie my secret knots
You're helping me discover who I am
To say what I think — and not give a damn.

It's only because
you are listening to me
that I have the chance
to express my daily thoughts
that would have been forgotten.

You're saying that Sherry is a real tease
She doesn't care about the men she knows
She doesn't go out of her way to please
Her availability is a pose
These poor guys will do anything for her
Lacking a clue of her indifference
She's turning love into a ligature
Their sincerity makes no difference
You don't appreciate her behavior
You're saying it reflects her bitterness
She's getting back at the guys who've hurt her
She's completely consumed with unhappiness
She's already divorced — three times over
Nothing's worse than a disgruntled lover.

Taking orders at
the café is the perfect
ploy for snaring the
unsuspecting fools who
eagerly keep showing up.

I feel some pressure to make things happen
I'm infatuated with this woman
Emotions kickstart my adrenaline
I want to be her only leading man
But she is talking to plenty of guys
While I'm stuck in my office by myself
With Bruce I'm beginning to empathize
Like him I feel deserted on a shelf
I'm building up the nerve to ask her out
I feel impelled to seize the momentum
I can't be inhibited by my doubts
I've got uncertainty to overcome
I just can't be quiet — I have to move
I've got my masculinity to prove.

The aching yearning
of love forced me to ask her
out on Friday night
and we'll be meeting at a
fancy Chinese restaurant.

I am beginning to feel the weight of
A sickening familiarity
She said yes — giving me more to dream of
This doesn't solve my insecurity
I'm anticipating our coming date
And imagining how she'll dress for me
Excited daydreaming is really great
It has the appearance of being carefree
But now my emotions are invested
I'm starting to yearn for certain results
Because I know nothing is guaranteed
Moderating myself is difficult
I want to see that she cares about me
This harrowing feeling won't let me be.

I'd like to wrench out
my insecurity and
be as casual
and as nonchalant as a
forgetful Lothario.

She does enjoy my sensitivity
Savoring my able conversation
She likes my easy creativity
I think I'm winning her admiration
She says she wants to keep talking to me
It helps to lessen her aggravations
She's feeling a taste of despondency
And experiencing wild gyrations
She's getting divorced and can't let it be
Her future income is a fixation
She does need money to live happily
Her love is worth some remuneration
She's not letting Bruce get off easily
She demands to be treated decently.

I do wish that she
would forget about Bruce as
obviously he's
a bully and a drunk and
how can that be attractive?

There's a paradox in liberation
At least of the type that I am seeking
Trying too hard creates separation
I'd like to give up the habit of grasping
There is the initial desperation
A lingering period of suffering
That's enough to inspire frustration
That culminates in a new beginning
From there what's needed is relaxation
A peace apart from unending striving
Fascination with subtle vibrations
There is patience to be cultivating
I want to surf with my motivations
I would like to balance with emanations.

Romantic love and
political victory
may be delusions
to be grasped only for a
moment before they dissolve.

Our evening together went splendidly
And it ended with a lingering kiss
Leaving me dreaming again hungrily
Thinking of ways that we could coalesce
She wants to keep on talking frequently
And again tomorrow in the morning
Which I'm looking forward to eagerly
To begin the day with our conversing
But something seems a little odd to me
I think I'm noting a little distance
She's parceling affections carefully
I'm getting a sense of some resistance
She is not as open as she could be
So I will play along and wait and see.

Our rendezvous on
the phone as I'm lying
in my bed and she's
sitting up drinking coffee
isn't quite enough for me.

Do people fall in love — and recover?
I wonder why we use the word "falling"
Like jumping out of a plane together
To experience a weightless floating?
This changes my sense of reality
Fixing my attention on a lover
Perhaps it's happening naturally
Involving obstacles to get over
Passion is taking so much attention
I don't want to live like this everyday
It is a constant and stressful tension
Straining to find exciting things to say
And my lingering doubts won't let me be
That perhaps she is only teasing me.

The necessary
details of getting through the
ordinary chores
of my daily life do make
me increasingly weary.

She says on the phone that she enjoys me
She suspects I don't know my influence
That I have an intriguing history
And sometimes my words cast a kind of trance
That I'm not like the other guys she's known
There's depth and breadth that is exceptional
And that when her thoughts won't let her alone
I'm helping her to be more flexible
It's true — each situation is unique
And can be viewed from different angles
There are various solutions to seek
When stubborn attitudes are untangled
But most of all she likes my gentle touch
And she likes my attention very much.

She doesn't know the
influence she's having on
me as I struggle
with my equanimity
and with love's uncertainty.

I do find myself imagining how
I am appearing to the one I love
And I'm guessing what she's thinking somehow
Contemplating the traits that I'm proud of
Replaying words we've spoken together
Taking encouragement in things she's said
Assessing the words that really matter
I could have said something better instead
I've turned her into a mirror of me
And I'm imagining what she's feeling
But I don't know if our passions agree
My distorted image is confusing
I'm lost in a hall of funhouse mirrors
The more I think — they're not getting clearer.

I just know that
I'm trying too hard to make
things happen that are
beyond my control and that
I really have to relax.

—*Tekkan*

Book III

I called several times with no response
And sent several text messages too
I'm adopting a pose of nonchalance
While stymied and wondering what to do
I suppose it's my responsibility
To make the first moves and see what happens
While working on my insecurity
I may have to surrender my passion
Girls are like buses — another's coming
It's not a benefit to care so much
Our predawn calls were encouraging
But now once again we are out of touch
I have got to accept the way things are
This crazy situation is bizarre.

With a head-turning
woman like her I'd always
be wondering who
else she is talking to
and I will not live like that.

I am on a quest to discover love
I'm feeling pressure to make things happen
What she's doing I have no control of
While I get these bursts of adrenaline
I am on edge and it's sharp and jagged
And I don't know why she's being aloof
I don't like being purposely ignored
I'm not surprised that I'm not shatterproof
As I search my thoughts for explanations
I struggle with my curiosity
Suffering now for my expectations
I'd like a little reciprocity
I'm a victim of my aspirations
Solitude feels like asphyxiation.

Yeah I know that I'm
putting myself under a
massive amount of
pressure but why the hell is
she choosing not to reply?

Hello my ridiculous gyrations
You're putting me through the wringer today
With unobtainable aspirations
I'll figure this out on another day
I'm better than this — I know my value
I am not going to let you scramble my head
This crazy passion is just a snafu
So I'll think about something else instead
I'm not going to let you agitate me
I know how to meditate and be calm
Practicing serenity is my key
I know your essence — you are a pipe bomb
I'm disbelieving you my demon doubt
On another day I'll figure this out.

The lotus posture
is my dissolving machine
moving energy
along my spine through my limbs
dissipating crazy thoughts.

I know she is a social butterfly
She has plenty of opportunity
I don't know what her absence signifies
I'm not enjoying my passivity
I am going to return to match.com
Female company is available
Loneliness is a fragmentation bomb
Doing nothing isn't acceptable
I've done it before — I know what to do
I'll leave a hundred messages today
There are all these profiles to go through
And I'm certain to get some interplay
Most won't respond — but I really don't care
Nothing is happening if I don't dare.

I'm able to be
indifferent about the
massive numbers of
women online until I
get a glimpse of who they are.

During college I read a short story
About a guy with a beautiful wife
The emotion of the tale was heavy
Showing the cataclysm of his life
His wife began to drift away from him
With a separation of affection
For no reason weightier than a whim
She never gave him an explanation
She just stopped talking and left him alone
When confronted all she did was to weep
At the end of the tale his wife was gone
He had a terrible time trying to sleep
It is odd that she was the one weeping
And yet it was he who wasn't sleeping.

Who knows what really
happened between the couple
and it's possible
important facts were left out
but I feel sorry for him.

I do love listening to Alan Watts
He's a master of ancient Eastern wisdom
He's helping me with my consciousness knots
Feeding my craving for mysticism
The point of his talk is liberation
I listen to him while driving my car
His words propose a cosmic flirtation
On occasion he will reference a star
He says the star and I are related
Our existence depends on each other
Though the connections are complicated
It's true that we are woven together
I am waiting for that bolt of lightning
A change of view that is enlightening.

Alan says the more
I seek for liberation
the further away
I thrust it from me because
it cannot be seized by force.

Alan's temperament is humorous
He jokes about a goose in a bottle
There is a point — he's not gratuitous
The plight of the goose is a boondoggle
So how can we get the goose out alive?
The Zen master is stubbornly silent
There's no solution that we can contrive
It doesn't help to become more strident
The master takes another direction
It seems he's forgotten about the goose
He's even joyful in misdirection
And then he exclaims that the goose got loose
It just happened without explanation
Maybe because of its relaxation?

Alan's tale about
the Zen master and the goose
is reassuring
about liberation and
a lover's befuddlement.

Alan talks about Hindu mythmaking
He dwells upon the game of hide and seek
The Gods are laughing — the Gods are dancing
They hide their faces and then — take a peek
But how does this comport with suffering?
When we squirm and strain to escape our pain?
When the impact of life is confusing?
It's hard to determine what's most humane
Alan talks about the game of our dreams
Soon enough we'd be bored with paradise
Constant happiness is not what it seems
Perhaps our troubles are a kind of spice
We couldn't know happiness without strife
Having hardships gives meaning to a life.

The intensity
the suffering may be too
much to be borne and
yet the game continues on
perhaps to awakening.

The unhindered mind is spontaneous
With thought following thought following thought
And often they are miscellaneous
But my dilemmas come in getting caught
Liberation need not be difficult
As long as I'm not picking and choosing
When I'm yearning for a certain result
And that is when I will be suffering
Then how does one love and also succeed
With desire approaching possession?
Because I'd like to be spreading my seeds
And I'm cultivating a fixation
This girl is dangling just beyond my reach
And I'm so focused on winning my peach.

I am lingering
on the point of frustration
while practicing the
spiritual jujitsu of
a tricky relaxation.

I love the sound that a temple bell makes
It strikes the air with reverberations
It is an invitation to awake
It serves to quiet anticipations
The bell has a tone of solemnity
Which for me is also deeply joyful
It has an odd familiarity
Even though I am anxious and doubtful
It says loving peace is available
And I don't have to get what I'm seeking
When something better is obtainable
It points to an overall releasing
There's a hint that I've known such peace before
I already have what I'm looking for.

The temple bell speaks
of an underlying and
invigorating
simplicity of joyful
being just beyond yearning.

I'm living beyond the temple's borders
And all caught up with winning and losing
I'm worried about what's around the corner
And hungering for objects of my choosing
I'm dangling by a string of my desires
And the wind is making a toy of me
I'm swaying back and forth over a fire
And feeling how my thoughts are scorching me
All I have to do is simply relax
And release what I think that I must get
It is such an insanely simple act
Part of me doesn't want to do it yet
I am a fool living a comedy
Playing a part in greater harmony.

Laughing at myself
I guess is part of the game
rules as long as I'm
not taking my dilemmas
so very seriously.

Messages of peace are all around me
I love listening to wind in the leaves
It is a gentle sound of harmony
I am hearing it tumble sigh and heave
It is a sermon given wordlessly
It's really OK if I have to grieve
And to feel my emotions heartily
As they are signals for me to receive
The *dharma* functions mysteriously
I feel it when I'm listening to trees
Releasing is a possibility
I can free myself and live at my ease
All this striving is an absurdity
It is not helping and can only tease.

Relaxing is the
hardest trick for me pull
off and I do it
when I'm not even thinking
about the need to relax.

I get a sense that I shouldn't hold on
And that I shouldn't be yearning for her
There's a possibility that she's gone
And I can't get back to the way things were
Any master I've heard of can let go
They don't fight against their circumstances
They imitate the water and they flow
I am trying to accept her absence
Sometimes I wonder what she's doing now
And I have to let my mind think like this
I know these thoughts will dissipate somehow
As I am remembering our last kiss
It's funny how my thoughts are like the wind
And when I fight I summon a whirlwind.

My mind and my heart
will whirl as they do until
exhaustion taking
however long it takes and
I have to let it happen.

Once again you snare me with a surprise
I didn't expect you to call again
I forgot you know how to dramatize
I am reluctant but I can't refrain
Only you would ring me at 5 a.m.
No one else would think of calling me then
I'd say I'm not happy — but yes I am
I'd thought we'd connect but didn't know when
You give me an excuse that I can't believe
You say you're paralyzed by the divorce
And you say that I can give you relief
Because you're taking on your ex's force
Your ex-husband is being malicious
And our conversations are delicious.

I'm getting a hint
that this girl has me wrapped
around her pinky
finger and I'm a fool who
couldn't be happier.

The Buddha is said to have remembered
All of his past lives including when he
Was a dolphin which must have reappeared
To him perhaps as one of his happy
Incarnations while I can't see beyond
The boundaries of this apprehensive
Human being which to me is a bond
That is sometimes hard involving pensive
Episodes and I am imagining
What life would be like if I were a stag
Living under the sun and moon roaming
Amid the woods and fields without a lag
Between my sensations and perceptions
With much less complicated decisions.

I am sure there would
be competition with the
other stags over
does but there would also be
much frolic in my swiftness.

The humidity is evident as
Soon as I rise from bed and the air
Is cool early in the morning and has
A tangible liquid quality compared
To what it is in the depth of winter
When I am compelled to use lip balm to
Keep my lips from cracking and it's better
To spread lotion on my skin as I do
To prevent my skin from itching so I
Really do love summer when I may lounge
About the house with all the windows wide
Open without the hinderance to scrounge
For a few moments of natural warmth
Which is a benefit of summer's worth.

By about the mid-
point of afternoon the heat
will begin to sear
the moisture in the air and
everything begins to cook.

Day after day the sun in the summer
Often appears by itself in the sky
And its corona is a bright glimmer
Of white-hot heat which makes everything dry
Despite the humidity — if there are
Many days without the refreshment of
Rain then the yards of grass do become charred
Which is a part of summer I don't love
And last night the sky was cracking with peals
Of thunder and flashing with lightning bolts
Which made the phenomenal sky surreal
Dimming and lighting with electric volts
But today there's no evidence about
Of any rain and we are in a drought.

A couple of days
ago the sunset was a
brilliant orange as
a result of the wildfires
combusting in Canada.

Because I am a sincere person who
Usually does do the right thing and
I may slip into self-righteousness too
I do make a lot of mistakes offhand
And later on I think about what I
Did and I'm excessively critical
Of myself thinking I am a bad guy
Not wanting to be hypocritical
Then I'm looking in a funhouse mirror
And all my features and behaviors are
Distorted and my self-image shimmers
Which is a state that is very bizarre
And then I know there's something I should do —
I had better relax — or I am blue.

It's much easier
to do what I gotta do
while forgetting my
self-image which is not
something that's easy to do.

I share my house with a liberated
Being whom I have named Kitcat and he
On occasion can be frustrated
But he is happy ordinarily
His motivations aren't calculated
He thinks and acts instantaneously
Some of the time he is animated
For the bulk of the day he is sleepy
He certainly can be agitated
But I never doubt his sincerity
He's not in the least bit fabricated
He flows with a blissful simplicity
I don't think he's ever been dejected
He's much more likely to be elated.

For some reason he
will suddenly scamper
through the house as fast
as he can without ever
asking for permission first.

I have an uneasy relationship
With the system governing the nation
As our rulers do resort to their whips
To compel behavior to their notions
Which revolve around dividing people
Into perpetrators and rescuers
And victims using a trick that appeals
To our self-pity which is quite sincere
And the trick works because of the use of
Malefactors who need to be defeated
Which rescuers do because of their love
And the agitation is repeated
Ceaselessly because it is so easy
To play the victim and to be lazy.

What would people do
if they realized
they are playing each
of the roles in turn?

Perhaps it's obvious that any way
Of governing a mass of people will
Involve tricks and coercion to convey
Some peace hopefully without overkill
But this is a human predicament
To which I'd rather not devote too much
Thought as I don't want to become hellbent
On winning the argument inasmuch
As squabbling and suffering doesn't
Ever end and I'd rather find my peace
In sincere companionship that isn't
Based on leverage but that brings release
In the awareness and acceptance of
My craziness — as I'm looking for love.

I do need friends who
can occasionally put
disagreements out
of mind as opinions are
needlessly combustible.

She is my maybe lover who wants to
Talk to me on the phone every morning
At 5 a.m. which I've fallen into
Because I think that I may be getting
Somewhere with her but I'm not at all sure
Because at times she will disappear and
And then I am crestfallen and unsure
That we'll ever talk again and I'm stunned
When she comes back into my life again
With a flimsy excuse usually
Having to do with her divorce that strains
Credulity but she talks beautifully
And she has a way of hooking me that
Works — I don't know what to do about that.

I've convinced
myself our talking at
odd hours is harmless
and inconsequential.

I am not without my defenses as
I'm relying on my meditation
And deploying nonchalance with the jazz
Engaging in bantering flirtation
And if you could see me lying in bed
As I am speaking to her you would see
A guy in his element spouting threads
Of ebullient curiosity
Dissecting the absurdities of our
Society and yes I am talking to
Her deep in conversation for an hour
But I could speak to anyone and do
The same as I am a guy who is free
And as casual as I want to be.

And yet she could go away
And I wouldn't get my way
And that would be bad
And I would be sad
But really what can I say?

As I ride my bicycle down a length
Of mostly unused asphalt road every
Afternoon pedaling in the wavelength
Of the summer sun which can be hazy
I can see dozens of grasshoppers on
The road and they are startled by my bike
And they are a surprise to come upon
As everyone will jump and some will strike
Me as I'm passing by and they don't hurt
And I find the phenomenon funny
Which I can't do anything to avert
In summer on asphalt when it's sunny
As this is the season for grasshoppers
In autumn — woolly bear caterpillars

In autumn woolly
bear caterpillars on the
asphalt undulate
across and along my way
but they don't see me at all.

Summer is the time for being lazy
So this poem won't be important and
I can't focus when the air is hazy
So I might as well be sleepy and bland
And write about nothing which is not as
Easy as it might seem as I do need
To be sufficiently careful whereas
If I weren't no one would bother to read
These words and that would be a blow to my
Ego and so today I will confess to you
That for years I've been intending to buy
A hummingbird feeder which I would do
For entertainment but I am lazy
Especially when the air is hazy.

It's so simple to
put up a feeder to see
the hummingbirds but
I haven't got around to
doing it as of today.

As I'm lying awake in bed idly
Waiting for 5 a.m. I can listen
Half-heartedly lackadaisically
To the distant hum of the traffic when
I discover the birds have stopped singing
As they did in spring and I guess they are
Done with mating and summer is bringing
An absence I haven't noticed before
So I keep myself occupied looking
At the clock and listening to the sounds
Of people moving about and driving
Wherever they are going around town
And doing whatever it is they do
Generating an echo as they go.

I'm just waiting for
the clock to get to
5 a.m. when I'll call
and hear her say my name
again and then we'll converse.

I am not as captivated as I
Was and I am practicing nonchalance
With a better estimation of why
We are talking so much in response
To an emptiness and seeing what can
Be done with words at an odd hour of
The day which is perhaps better now than
Not talking in imitation of love
With lighthearted exploration minus
Any expectations of entangled
Consequences as our chat is about
Cavorting with innovative angles
Making a festival of all of our doubts
So we are playing with patterns of words
And being serious would be absurd.

However much we
affect each other I am
able to attend
to my livelihood without
bewildering illusions.

When rushing on the highway it's common
To see the fields of corn or soybeans in
August but today I saw the awesome
Sight of a field of sunflowers wherein
A multitude of yellow faces piqued
My interest with their curious stance
Blossoming at the peak of summer heat
Which I appreciated in a glance
As a blandishment of summer with a
Blazing sun hanging in the sky keeping
Steady pace with my speeding car with the
Army of yellow faces emerging
And vanishing while bringing a smile to
My face which is a lovely thing to do.

Without a word the
sunflowers in serried ranks
gaze patiently up
at the exuberance of
the vibrant summer sunshine.

Please indulge me as I engage my wit
Gathering a ridiculous group of
Words which may in fact entirely fit
Wherein each line follows the one above
Weaving with a semblance of logic which
Gives the impression of progress to a
Satisfying conclusion with a pitch
Inciting curiosity in the
Meaning of words and the significance
Of the ceaseless parading of events
Which is important that it does make sense
Otherwise it wouldn't be worth a cent
As there is a worthiness in spinning puns
Anticipating the punchline is fun.

Can there be sincerity
Coupled with veracity
Pulling you along
With a little song
Leading to serenity?

I need to find a posture that helps to
Keep me balanced and happy even when
I lose a friend and don't know what to do
Because I know the value of a friend
So with an end of communication
Without a reason I can understand
I do feel a familiar frustration
In a feeling of isolation and
I don't believe it's helpful to evade
A sense of loss or to engage in a
Fit of anger or to become afraid
That somehow I am unworthy of the
Solicitude of a friend and so then
I can boomerang and begin again.

I don't believe that
I'm the only one who has
accumulating
grief that disguises itself
under other emotions.

This is the tipping point of the year when
The air in the morning is cool and comes
In through my open windows and yet then
The afternoons are sweltering on some
Days and the heat is beastly which isn't
A condition a person enjoys but
Unconsciously adapts to and doesn't
Notice or bellyache about but what
Does get to me is when I drive about
Town and I can see in scattered patches
The first touches of autumn leaves without
A doubt and every year the sight catches
Me because it points in the direction
Of February and disaffection.

I suffer from a
syndrome called
post-traumatic
February disorder
and can't be talked
out of it.

I am trudging on the road to happy
Destiny putting my faith in a net
Of ancient ideas that I believe
And without knowing what I'm doing yet
I am following the resonance of
My heart which says that each of us is an
Imperishable imbecile of love
Beyond knowing how the journey began
And hemmed about with a forgetfulness
Doing my wholehearted best on this day
And flirting with liberation I guess
But when it is coming I cannot say
Recalling a message that it's easy
Like relaxing within a peaceful breeze.

The way is easy
as long as I do my best
and not worry at
all about the outcome of
everything that I may do.

She likes to go to garage sales and I
Went along with her in the afternoon
And we explored the rolling countryside
As I wanted the chance to be in tune
With her with the casual passage of
Time within the close confines of a car
Even though I really don't share her love
For buying things — we did find a bazaar
Where I bought a pair of cowboy boots and
I don't remember what she got as I
Just wanted to be with her somewhat stunned
When she suddenly wanted to drive by
All the bars where her ex-husband drinks to
See if he was inside and drinking too.

She had me driving
to places I had never
been to and wouldn't
ever return to as I
explored her quirky habits.

Her not being able to let go of
Where her ex-husband is or what he may
Be doing is a signal to me of
A crazy fixation as much to say
That she's obsessed with him and can't let go
Which means that she's thinking more about him
Than me which I've suspected even though
She is with me now the chances are slim
That I'll be the guy she's dreaming about
Especially while she's consumed with her
Failed marriage even though he's a lout
So I'm beginning to think she prefers
Abuse mixed in with excitement perhaps
Which I think clearly leads to a collapse.

Presently she is
like a loaf of half-baked bread
and the yeast has to
be left alone to do its work
before there can be flavor.

What am I going to do now that I can
See that I am not the center of her
Attention and I need to have a plan
That's sensibly based on what I prefer
Because I like her company and as
I am engaged in a fantasy of
Possessing her — so should I quit? Whereas
I love the feeling of being in love
And maybe we can keep talking without
Doing any harm to each other or
Mostly to me if I can figure out
How to hang in there and open the door
To the possibility of love — or
To keep her from becoming a big chore?

There is curiosity
Inside our verbosity
Involving some clues
Of what we could do
With some reciprocity.

This is a quiet thunder rumbling from
A distance and it has soft edges and
A gentle touch not like a booming drum
And not like the sudden claps and cracks and
The tearing of the sky that I have heard
But instead it is so grand and wondrous
Which is difficult to put into words
When definitions are superfluous
And this thunder does mean something to me
As it reveals an echoing vastness
Of horizons I'm not able to see
Of mysteries concealed by the darkness —
This thunder is casting a soothing spell
It is a summons like a temple bell.

Also the patter
of continuing rain has
a gentle cadence
coming through open windows
carried along in a breeze.

My experience now is to watch the
Ups and downs of my daily life and to
Know when I'm not at my best and that a
New circumstance is arriving to do
Whatever it will to change my mood and
I realize that I can't wrench myself
Into a better mood but that I can
Learn to surf emotions as life itself
Is a continuing vibration of
Ups and downs much like the crests and the troughs
Of waves and I will weather my share of
Disappointment and success and slough off
The weight of serious expectations
And learn to live with my fluctuations.

It's easy to talk
this way but there's a trick in
really living this
way which involves letting go
of serious assumptions.

This habit I have of writing sonnets
Is kind of crazy and doesn't make sense
As I can't see that I'll ever profit
Financially and I have no pretense
Of doing more than just playing with words
Putting them together in odd ways and
Deploying irony may be absurd
Upsetting expectations if I can
By relying on my sincerity
Traipsing in a definite direction
Practicing my verbal dexterity
Not caring about remuneration
Because — as much as you — I want to see
What this crazy poem is going to be.

Don't ask me how this
poem is going to finish
because I haven't
a clue until I blunder
on a happy finale.

The birds are not as noisy as they were
During their springtime exuberance as
The mating season is done and they are
Liberated now and have much less sass
About defending their territory
But they can be heard now and again as
In sporadic joyful oratory
And they do lighten my heart as I pass
Setting me free from the clutch of my thoughts
And the birds are often invisible
Hidden in foliage but I can spot
Them in the air when I'm able
To absorb myself in my surroundings
And attending to birds is a wingding.

Foliage hides
the absolutely
unique twisting
of each branch.

I'm not liberated because I'm still
Engaged in pursuit of this woman who
Knows very well that I'm obsessed and will
Call her every morning and join her too
At least once a week for lunch or supper
In restaurants or cafés and a day
Ago I drove her to a carpet store
As I'm doing my best to find a way
To insinuate my presence into
Her life and it's all very well for the
Buddha to be autonomous and to
Not be concerned about results in a
Meditative state of serenity
But I do want her reciprocity.

She says she talks to
me more than to anyone
else in her life and
that's the sort of comment that
keeps me so interested.

The other day she recruited me with
Several other big guys to move her
Oak armoire which was such a heavy lift
Out of her ex's house and up the stairs
To her townhouse and I was the guy on
The left front of it and to pull it up
To strain my back and legs to come upon
One more step above without giving up
And in between each heave its weight would drop
With a prodigious thud and it almost
Smashed my foot but we made it to the top
After I had expended my utmost
Energy and I am glad that it is done
Because there are other ways to have fun.

The ordeal was
another way for me to
ingratiate my
potency into her good
graces — at least I hope so.

It's a question when I'm assembling
Words whether I'm giving preference to
My ears or eyes as I will be saying
Words over again and listening to
The way they tickle my ears and also
I will be counting syllables to put
A pleasing number within each line so
I can measure every metrical foot
And I will be taking the time to rhyme
Coming at the end of every line but
It is not my habit at every time
To be obvious and so to see what
I am doing you have to read the words
To discover whether they are absurd.

If there isn't a
sufficiently pleasing thread
of meaning to keep
you following me you would
stop listening or reading.

I've got to carry on with this girl and
Not give a damn whether what I want comes
About or not as I do what I can
And am learning at least a little some
Of the ploys involved in being relaxed
And passionate at the same time and how
I can do that and not become attached
To the results is a trick that somehow
Comes along perhaps only through doing
Exactly what I'm doing and it might
Be more propitious to be taking
More time to see whether she is the right
One for me as there are indications
That she likes to perpetrate frustrations.

Being together
doesn't necessarily
mean that we are
getting somewhere or
will arrive together.

Kitcat is perilous like a tiger
He doesn't care that he's only pint size
Extending no more than a foot lengthwise
I know him to be a ready biter
With the inclination of a fighter
He stares ferociously with tiger's eyes
With an intensity to hypnotize
Taut and tense in every nervy fiber
While he knows my habits — and I know his
I sing him tunes of nonsense quality
He flops on the floor and shows his belly
Does he want to play? He certainly does
He's quite capable of frivolity
And I know his belly feels like jelly.

He has the ferocity
Along with sinuosity
Pouncing with pleasure
He's very clever
But he lacks verbosity.

I've not been one to follow conventions
Instead I've taken odd romantic jobs
Shorn of the dignity preferred by snobs
I know I cherish certain pretensions
That come with a load of expectations
One can't seek clarity and be a slob
Or cater to the whims of vicious mobs
I want to be clear in my intentions
And to play with words and make a living
Forgoing a rewarding salary
To linger with the inexpressible
To play with notions of awakening
Though my method may be a fallacy
I do aim to be comprehensible.

It may not be credible
Or even respectable
To try to profit
By writing sonnets
But it is delectable.

I do understand your emotions and
Know that you're having a difficult time
And seeking for balance in the meantime
Letting go of a marriage that has spanned
Maybe three decades and that you can't stand
Being dispensed with when you're in your prime
Which indicates a ton of loss and I'm
Not disoriented and am on hand
To divert the agitation of your
Thoughts with the exploration of my words
As there's no need to be stuck in the past
When you could be hopeful and open doors
And as I am you could be looking toward
A liberation and a peace that lasts.

Driving around to
bars to see whether his car
is parked outside
isn't fun and I'd rather
do anything else with you.

I get a boost talking to you every
Morning on the phone when most people are
Still sleeping in bed and it is bizarre
That we can be exchanging repartee
Consuming an hour in reverie
So who would care to get drunk in a bar
Or to be constantly picking at scars
And be writhing about in dependency
When intimacy alleviates so
Much of our compulsive agitation
And there's no substitute for feeling loved
Which I missed through years of living solo
And now that's ending with conversation
As you're making me feel understood.

Some days I wake up
early and count the minutes
until I can call
and hear again your cheerful
voice I am accustomed to.

The American soldier is so poorly
Appreciated by Americans
Who don't care much about Afghanistan
While soldiers take honor seriously
And they dedicate their lives to duty
As they follow orders and garrison
The most belligerent and distant land
Not questioning the nation's policy
But America suffers poor leadership
So blame the presidents and generals
And our governing class is terrible
Lost in petty venal partisanship
Where the blame-shifting is perennial
And their constant lies are contemptible.

The burden of our
nation's mistakes falls upon
honor-bound soldiers
and their families while the
elites appropriate wealth.

Arrogance and incompetence are on
The rise in American leadership
Coming with deceiving partisanship
In a news media that strings along
Narratives designed not only to con
Americans but also to equip
Politicians with propaganda stripped
Of heartfelt regard for the truth forgone
Because our intellectuals are more
Interested in power and control
And now Americans are bitterly
Divided which is harder to ignore
As every calamity takes a toll
And politicians fail repeatedly.

Righteous
propaganda
inspires
fellow-feeling in
everyone except
its targets.

I am a droplet of the universe
And I embody its propensities
For dissolution and ascendency
And I do determine the impetus
Of direction from the secret impulse
Of my thoughts that pivot incessantly
In a delicate dance tentatively
Balanced between the better and the worse
And I need to be aware when the tenor
Of my thinking is mostly negative
And I'm soliciting unhappiness
And then it helps very much to explore
The releasing of thoughts generative
Of a welcome relaxation and peace.

Circumstances do
impose leverage over
times but a watchful
and persisting gentleness
emboldens optimism.

I traveled to Ohio to visit
Relatives and to take my elderly
Mother to meet her sister tenderly
Reuniting the two from the limits
Of distance and time making explicit
All the buried memories heartily
At a surprise party sprung cheerfully
On my mother's sister and we did it
To celebrate her sister's 90th
Birthday and the sisters will have very
Much to talk and to reminisce over
And the moment of meeting took my breath
Watching their reunion became teary
With a wealth of liveliness left over.

Beloved husbands
children
grandchildren
great-grandchildren
the vanishing world —
so much to discuss.

The fingers and ankles and the balls of
The feet are vital components of a
Bicycle rider as I learned with the
Use of a light carbon fiber bike of
Superior quality with the shoes of
A different clip-on style and with the
Gear shifting mechanism needing a
Challenging and puzzling sequence of
Finger manipulation new to me
Which I had to remember on the fly
And my ankles are attuned to the twist
That frees the shoe from the pedal but I
Couldn't click into the pedal and missed
Much too often as I strove to apply
Directional pressure to get the gist.

My brother loaned me
the use of his best bike which
unexpectedly
demanded a different
display of dexterity.

I am a simple guy with a speedy
Aluminum bicycle at home but
My brother drives to distant trails and puts
His bikes on a rack on a luxury
Car and he can track his proximity
Heart rate and wind speed and I don't know what
Else but besides all that he has the guts
To ride like he's crazy repeatedly
Over the years and I was proud to keep
Up and surprised that I could fixing my
Attention on him because suddenly
He'd race and the rivers and trees would sweep
By but after several good hours I
Did get tired and moved exhaustedly.

Days later he sent
me an email with graphs of
elevation with
exact locations and a
sum of our average speed.

I am reading an Agatha Christie
Murder mystery about what appeared to
Be a double suicide having to
Do with a respectable and happy
Couple of British high society
Which occurred a decade previous to
The events of the story which turned to
An examination of memory
Involving insights gleaned from the British
Empire giving weight to the phrase that
"An elephant remembers" implying
That telling clues however diminished
Lie dormant within incomplete views that
Disparate people hold that need sifting.

Like the elephants
people cherish opinions
precariously
based on uncertain facts that
are disappearing targets.

The furrowed brow and comprehending eyes
Of elephants are curious clues to
A sensibility with a strange view
That implies that they surely could be wise
To predicaments and choices with ties
Of volatility of what to do
Within the circumstances leading to
Their haphazard impulses when surprised
And if the expression is true that the
Elephants remember the insults or
The generosity of people from
Years ago then they are truly due a
Sympathetic respect and a rapport
Earned from the mystery from which we come.

If I were born with
the trunk the enormous girth
the feet and the ears
of an elephant I would
cavort with lumbering strength.

It's better to admit that it's bigger
Than you and over time it will beat you
Down and will thoroughly discourage you
And you've heard enough lies to be bitter
And you do yourself damage to bicker
And after the divorce it's clear you're through
So what is it that you're trying to do?
As you know he's not a normal drinker
And an alcoholic won't get better
And if he's not willing to save himself
You know there is nothing that you can do
You're divorced — it's done — so be a quitter
It's way past time to take care of yourself —
I've reached a limit of what I can do.

You've got to admit
that you've hit a wall with him
there's nothing to do
other than to let him deal
with his alcoholism.

There is a way to get out of trouble
Whether a person is alcoholic
Or is one who loves an alcoholic
And it really is inevitable
And after it's done it's not a puzzle
You've got to admit that the guy is sick
And then surrendering becomes the trick
Then finally things are manageable
There just *has* to be an end to fighting
When every effort to control it flops
The only answer is relaxation
I know even though he might be dying
Your intention to cure it has to stop —
Try to let go of your expectations.

When I finally
admitted that I was an
alcoholic a
weight was lifted from my
shoulders and I became free.

She says — I went over to his house the
Very home where we raised our family
And I saw the mess of his apathy —
The counter was cluttered with dishes — the
Carpet was dirty — things were scattered — the
Dog was tense and ready to bite me —
There was a sense of unreality
With him sitting on the stairs and in a
Daze in his underwear before he had
To dress for work and seeing him like that
I thought he's not attractive anymore
And I couldn't be mad but sure was sad
To see the misery he's arrived at
With our history which I can't ignore.

And now I don't have
to be thinking about him
any more and I
can be free from whatever
compulsive needs I had.

I say that — I try to remember when
I'm sad or unhappy for whatever
Reason or when I'm feeling the pressure
Of being separate from people in
My life that the Eastern *Dharma* begins
With suffering and that I will suffer
Because of my stubbornness whenever
I can't let go of something but I can
Remember and see the simplicity
Of the point that if I'm not clinging to
What I want then I won't be suffering
But I admit I have difficulty
Doing my best at letting go — and to
Be better at that I am practicing.

Doing my best while
letting go of results is
a propitious
trick of relaxation that
I haven't begun to master.

I can't practice very well on my own
And I need people who share at least some
Of the ideas I'm using who can come
To understanding me and to be shown
How better it is than being alone
And I think you know where I'm coming from
And I'm telling you that it means a ton
To be listening to you on the phone
As we both know from experience that
Alcoholism is deadly and there's
So much more to be had from life than to
Be isolated and lonely in what
Is certain to become a mess that spares
No misery — not knowing what to do.

If what I say sounds
crazy imagine how things
would be if I had
no one to mitigate the
nonsense inside of my head.

I catch myself at odd moments saying
To myself when nobody but me is
Listening that "she is my girl" and is
This really true as I am suspecting
That my subconsciousness is asserting
That "she is my girl" and in fact she does
Love me and in idle moments she does
Care for me as much as I am caring
About her? But perhaps it's true that by force
Of will I am repeating a guess that
I desperately hope to be the truth
When I know deep down that I can't enforce
My wishes on reality and that
I may be fooling myself with half-truths.

I do have to watch
such messages when part of
me is trying to
convince the other part they're
true — when they may not be true.

There was the nagging incident when I
Waited at a restaurant for 40
Minutes alone for her and she hardly
Expressed a reason and as a nice guy
I didn't quibble wanting to get by
Without unpleasantness — and again we
Were at a restaurant being carefree
Having a good time when things went awry
When she saw a man she knew before and
Invited him to join us unmindful
Of my feelings and the two of them were
Eagerly engaged excluding me and
I do admit that I was resentful
Lonely frustrated and doubtful of her.

Another time she
spoke to a waiter about
me in a manner
that wasn't quite respectful
as I sat by stoically.

When we meet together in public there
Is a good chance that we'll have fun and that
I'll drive home satisfied and thinking that
The night couldn't have gone better aware
Of emotional burdens that she bears
But sometimes it's true that I'm feeling flat
With worries that I don't want to look at
With nagging suspicions it may be fair
To question her regard for me and yet
When we speak on the phone before the dawn
Every day I am able to express
My heartfelt words and then I do forget
My doubts because of the joy I live on
Because conversation feels like success.

The facility
of expression that we share
in morning hours
has in it for me the joy
of being comprehended.

A spasm of the neck afflicted her
When she was alone in her living room
Which was a sharp searing pain I assume
While I was on my bike and nowhere near
And perhaps it felt like a sudden tear
And afterwards there was persisting gloom
Which she felt in the emergency room
As being old isn't easy for her
And so I was called to the hospital
I noticed she was well attended to
But my mother was weary and confused
She isn't moving well and she's brittle
So we have a course of treatment to do
And another stage of life is opened.

There were episodes
in the past with spasms in
her back that she's been
able to overcome so
there's reason to be hopeful.

I've noticed it and perhaps you have too
That dust accumulates inside a house
It would be helpful to have a loving spouse
There is so much maintenance to do
With little nagging chores to get through
And I have no remedy to espouse
No easy revelation to announce
There are some adjustments to attend to
When one of a married couple dies first
There was the joy of many loving years
Looked back upon with appreciation
Then suddenly that time of life is burst
And we are presented with strange new cares
Can we make a reevaluation?

My mom was always
the quiet underlying
security of our
family cooking suppers
and civilizing her kids.

I had an idea — but forgot it
I had it — but I'm not remembering
Now I'm stuck and sitting here questioning
Sometimes I suspect I'm losing my wits
Perhaps by now I'm only a half-wit
I was in the habit of note-taking
Reading a note is reawakening
But I've been lazy and not doing it —
You see it's so important to be on
The lookout for the spark of insight that
Springs a poem and when it comes I need to
Recognize it appreciate it on
The spot and seize on the catalyst that
Makes possible all the hullabaloo.

It's like entering
a room and realizing
you have forgotten
why you came — inspiration
slips quickly through my fingers.

Agatha Christie is an expert at
Revealing a person's character with
A quirk of speech in her dialogues with
A spice of intriguing happenings that
Impels me to keep reading even at
A time of night when I'd be sleeping with
My dreams as she is a maestro wordsmith
Who makes me jealous dangling her clues that
May amount to nothing or not but there
Are too many clues mixed with the details
Of plot to keep track of and I truly
Love her depiction of the British where
Subtle class distinctions make for blackmail
Within the rank of high society.

She reveals the
weakness and the meanness in
the disorder of
human nature directing
motivation to murder.

Agatha Christie clued me into the
Fact that I am a "dipsomaniac"
Which is a word meaning alcoholic
Which says I'm a "dipso" added to a
"Mania" which means I could be a
"Maniac" which is quite a verbal whack
Which implies people like me need smacks
To keep us soberly sensible in a
 World that expects much better of us
And I'm not going to quibble about that
As we have maniacal qualities
But I am not a dilophosaurus
Which was a toothy dinosaur that
Had much worse antisocial qualities.

Agatha Christie
uses her verbosity
quite responsibly
and she only had to use
the word once to make her point.

My house which I have almost finished paying
For is looking a little worse for wear and
The joints between my pipes are leaky and
I've put up with it for a while thinking
That my iron pipes will be expanding
Because colder weather is coming and
Isn't that what iron does when cold and
I saw how stupid I was admitting
I had to call a plumber reluctantly
Because I'm stingy but I did make the call
For a plumber and he said that pipes will
Leak and then he got to work and quickly
Discovered that a rubber hose had caused all
The mess which he fixed and gave me a bill.

I am a wordy
intellectual who could
convince himself that
iron pipes will expand in
cold and therefore stop the leaks.

I received an email today about
The Sistine Chapel which included a
Virtual tour which presented me a
Panoramic view and I could check out
The exquisite designs and expand out
The smallest details with a flick of the
Wrist and with a shift of the mouse of a
Mac computer which is nothing to pout
About and the email informed me that
Pope Julius became impatient with
Michelangelo because he believed
The artist was too dilatory at
The job and so the Pope questioned him with
Pique: Why was he so slow at what he did?

Michelangelo
answered Pope Julius
by saying that he
was still learning —
"*Ancora Imparo.*"

Now we have entered into September
Which does make me somewhat melancholy
I'm a little sad — but not unhappy
As I'm at an age when I remember
All the many times we've turned this corner
Maybe I am prematurely sappy
A little somber — though not unhappy
This isn't the darkness of December
There will be plenty of warm days to come
I'll ride my bike as often as I can
And savor every change of the season
By watching the quality of the sun
And noticing its diminishing span
As summer is reaching its completion.

The glare of the sun
is diminishing in the
evening and the light
touching my cottonwood leaves
has a golden glow about it.

In the affairs of state involving the
Conduct of warfare and of strategy
It's painful to perceive complacency
And negligence in the betters of a
Republic who wouldn't when they had the
Time order their plans with competency
So at the point of crisis they betray
Citizens and faithful allies and the
Families of our warriors even
In the event surrendering people
Into the clutches of the enemy
Unto death whatever one believes in
When our leaders lie it's contemptible
To covet power without decency.

Thousands of faithful
allies and American
citizens were left
behind in Afghanistan
by America's betters.

The dwelling where my family lived for
Most of my childhood is on the north hill
Of Stillwater and so the rooms are filled
With memories almost forgotten or
Over the verge of consciousness stored
Latently somehow within me but still
Available being bygone until
A turn of my thinking opens a door
For instance when I notice an object
Among hundreds of other objects that
Returns to present awareness a tang
Of emotional insight that connects
Whomever I was with who I am that
Delivers to me a walloping pang.

The oak rocking chair
In the living room where my Dad
used to watch football
on Sunday afternoons has
comfortable resonance.

My mom suffered a spasm of her neck
And now she can't turn her head to the left
She needs looking after and so I check
Whether she is eating and getting rest
The doctor prescribed her several pills
She needs reminding of when to take them
The pain in her head is making her ill
She's not defeated — just a little glum
But I am noticing that she's forgetful
She can't recall what happened yesterday
She eats so little that I get fretful
When I push her to eat she does give way
To get better she needs some directions
She doesn't have so many objections.

When awake she stays
bent over on the couch with
a hot or cold pack
pressed upon her neck as the
doctor has directed her.

The clouds are drifting to the south today
And the sky is filled with warm gentle light
And there was a hurricane yesterday
But not a hint of that in this sunlight
Much of America was torn by storm
So many houses were struck and destroyed
I do forget that such storms are the norm
And that tragedies are hard to avoid
The leaves today are suffused with the light
The glow of sun is blissfully peaceful
The turn toward autumn is beautifully bright
I have no reason to be regretful
The trouble is over the horizon
In the south it is hurricane season.

I would much rather
suffer the impending cold
and the blizzards of
Minnesota than the news
of another hurricane
brewing off of the Gulf Coast.

I've been noticing the patterns of birds
I saw a flock of sparrows yesterday
How can I capture them only with words?
We heard a boisterous blue jay today
The jay interrupted a Zoom meeting
And we absorbed it on a microphone
Most of my views of birds are fleeting
I see them flying between trees alone
Some days ago I saw a chickadee
On my bicycle I spotted a gull
There are turkey vultures in twos and threes
I don't believe I've heard a vulture's call
So many birds will be migrating soon
They will be returning again in June.

Toucans flamingos
Galápagos penguins and
various parrots
are birds that never venture
to frozen Minnesota.

She's wearing a bright yellow summer dress
With a string top exposing her shoulders
It's apparent she's dressing to impress
Stimulating an urge to embrace her
I'm guessing excitement can be helpful
Prompting me to be alert and fluent
To play with my words — and to be cheerful
I'm even able to experiment
To venture a little pleasing teasing
Hinting at her availability
Expressing that she's very appealing
That she could well be another Sherry
In response she's very animated
This is better than anticipated.

The Kung Pao Chicken
with spicy chili sauce and
with green onions and
with red chili peppers went
by without much noticing.

The dwelling where my family lived for
Most of my childhood is on the north hill
Of Stillwater and so the rooms are filled
With memories almost forgotten or
Over the verge of consciousness stored
Latently somehow within me but still
Available being bygone until
A turn of my thinking opens a door
For instance when I notice an object
Among hundreds of other objects that
Returns to present awareness a tang
Of emotional insight that connects
Whomever I was with who I am that
Delivers to me a walloping pang.

The oak rocking chair
In the living room where my Dad
used to watch football
on Sunday afternoons has
comfortable resonance.

Benji came to the park for our meeting
In a jacket with fabric around his
Neck with jeans and a ball cap and he does
Appear more bundled up which is fitting
As it is September and it's turning
Colder but then I wonder why he is
Wearing sandals without socks and I quiz
Him on his incongruity asking
Wouldn't his mostly bare feet defeat the
Purpose in choosing mostly warmer clothes?
And he remarks that he's stubborn and won't
Give in to the weather yet which is a
Belligerent attitude I share though
He thinks he is sensible — but I don't.

Cold air and bare feet
make my whole body chilly
but Benji may be
different and through force of
will he can stymie the cold.

On my bicycle gravity gets to
Hurt me on the hill to Houlton when I
Take the strain in my anguished breath and I
Expend the strength of body and heart to
Keep my legs going to raise my head to
Glimpse the crest before I lower my eyes
Because it's much easier not to try
To look above and it is better to
Stay in pace with my shadow on the hill
While my silhouette flexes before me
As my vision narrows as I'm going —
Eliminating stray thoughts is a skill
Moving single-pointedly is gutsy
Defeating the hill is satisfying.

Afterward in the
evening gravity gets to
punish me on the
couch as I recline and then
feel the strain of standing up.

Bison gave the Lakota everything
Said elder John Fire Lame Deer — and we used
His hide for our blanket our coat our bed —
Tipis and drums were made of skin — nothing
Was wasted — at night our drums were throbbing
Alive holy — with his stomach we made
Our soup kettle by dropping in a red-
Hot stone — and his skull with the pipe leaning
Against it was our sacred altar — his
Hooves became our rattles and his horns were
Our spoons — his sinews our bowstrings and thread —
His flesh strengthened us — became our flesh — his
Bones we made into knives — and his ribs were
Our children's sleds — and this is what you killed.

The greatest Sioux was
Tatanka Iyotake
Sitting Bull — when you
killed the bison you killed the
wild natural Indian.

I ask a question of a Zen master
"Where is the pathway to liberation?"
The master flips my expectations
He says "everyday mind" is the answer
At first it makes my footsteps easier
As I can make use of my frustrations
I don't have to strain at self-negation
And don't have to rush to get there faster
Ordinary perceptions are all that
I need as long as I'm attending to
What I am thinking — as it's happening —
The clues are here in what I'm looking at
There's nothing special that I have to do
Even mundane chores can be exciting.

The master says it
is outside of words
outside traditions
and there's nothing you
can do to grasp it.

Of course doing sonnets is just a game
That can't be compared with a hunt for truth
And I do sonnets because in my youth
I got caught up in William Shakespeare's fame
But how I'm doing it isn't the same
Because Shakespeare had to be quite a sleuth
With words without dictionaries for proof
Of the rightness of his words and to name
Phenomena with felicity as
He did far surpasses what I can do
And I'm relying on Rhymzone.com
On the Internet which readily has
So many suitable words easy to
Choose from — which I'm doing without a qualm.

I can't imagine
with my sloppy handwriting
using a pen and
relying on memory
to fashion each of my rhymes.

Imagine using a quill pen trying
Not to make any mistakes knowing that
Each page of paper is precious and that
What a waste it would be to be splotching
Its pristine quality by blundering
With ink and what could one do with a splat
But start over again while feeling flat
And then how absolutely frustrating
It would be to be wasting so much time
In repeating stupidly the same chore
Of attempting not to fumble again
And how would it be possible to rhyme
When the handwriting becomes such a bore
And mindless activity is a drain.

Back in the day the
fops paraded about town
wearing rapiers
which perhaps wasn't so good
for handwriting frustration.

When the sun is coming but hasn't yet
Risen over the horizon the trees
Are only black silhouettes and the leaves
Cast a darkness and it is hard to get
A view of details and the yard is set
In gloom and then slowly the shadows ease
And suddenly a wispy cloud is seized
In a pink light and then the grass looks wet
And drops of dew are shining on the hedge
And the needles of a pine are yellow
And swaths of leaves become brilliant with light
And each angle of the shed has an edge
And a few feathery clouds are mellow
And the sun behind the maple is bright.

A flock of tiny
birds flits between a dozen
trees and most of the
leaves are tinged in a slanting
light but there are still shadows.

It's difficult to talk about issues
With people who aren't attending to the
Small details of politics because the
Public rhetoric is just a tissue
Of lies and the reporters often choose
To take sides and so it's hard to find a
Common ground with people who don't have a
Clue when they put so much faith in the news
Which is tragically skewed — and it's tricky
For politicos because they want to
Be aggressive and not be defensive
And they fashion their lies without pity
For anyone they hurt because it's true
Domination is cruelly offensive.

Ordinary and
innocent people would be
abashed to learn how
many of their opinions
are based upon clever lies.

After the many poems I've written
I think it is possible that the point
Of what I'm doing may be out of joint
With you my readers as I've been bitten
By doing Zen by trying to fit in
A yen for liberation — to pinpoint
The moment of freedom in the midpoint
Of "everyday mind" as I believe in
The saying that each of us is Buddha
But we remain ignorant of the fact
So I am trying not to disappoint
You or exhaust you by leading you on a
Goose chase or by awarding you a sack
Of nothing as if it were a viewpoint.

Walking about on
the hunt for poetic
inspiration I've
been looking for freedom
in the writing of poems.

Genghis Khan was a brutal general
Coming from the steppes of Mongolia
He was the opposite of *Siddhartha* —
Was his vicious cavalry temporal?
Were his gory conquests ephemeral?
He wasn't *Avalokitesvara*
Who is a mythical *bodhisattva*
The Khan's ambitions were imperial —
The horse soldiers of Genghis Khan used bows
And arrows to lay waste to more land than
Any other ruler in history
And his clever brutality was so
Calamitous that his memory spans
Millennia in bloody infamy.

Somehow the hunt for
liberation coexists
with a primal lust
for viciousness that appears to
to be inexhaustible.

If you are one of those who don't turn
To a dictionary when they come to
An oddball word then you won't have a clue
About *bodhisattvas* — so why not learn?
It would only take a minute to earn
A propitious bit of wisdom new
To you on which you could happily chew
Over in your head as it's good to yearn
For a wider circumference of knowledge
And you could also easily look up
Avalokitesvara which I know
Is a puzzle to pronounce on the edge
Of absurdity — but why not shape up
Your vocabulary with some gusto?

You may not know that
Avalokitesvara
is an exalted
bodhisattva who has
one thousand busy hands.

When I got to Aldi's grocery store
I discovered that it was a sad day
Because no matter how much I would pay
I couldn't buy the thing that I adore
Because now they don't have it anymore
And there's really nothing that I can say
And why complain when it is just the way
That things are even though it is a bore
As there is a season for everything
And we have to endeavor to let go
Of succulent items on occasion
Otherwise we risk being ding-a-lings
And suffering is part of life — although
Patience becomes part of the equation.

Now I have something
to look forward to as it's
certain in June or
July watermelons will
be available again.

When the full moon is in the morning sky
It looks like a fixture stationary
Beyond the scattered clouds and it's very
Bright and as I'm absorbing the clouds I
Can see that they're transforming on the fly
As wind-blown wisps moving gradually
And I love to give my sight to airy
Sun lit visions because it breaks my ties
To the drama of my human world that
Never seems to cease for me on the ground
When my thoughts race one after another
But the sky shifts about at a pace that
Dissipates urgency and I'm not bound
To fixate on problems and be bothered.

There is nothing in
the sky to grab a hold of
and give context to
the fact the moon is moving
ceaselessly in an orbit.

Fran said that the swallows are mostly gone
Now and I've noticed that too when I'm on
My bike and so many others are on
The move and Fran says that they're being drawn
Southward not by the increasing cold on
The rise or by the darkness coming on
But because the food that they depend on
Becomes scarce in winter and that they're on
The fly at night so we don't see them go
And may not notice their absence — although
Because my head is in the clouds I know
By association of the outflow
Of the songbirds and I'm sad even though
I know that they'll be back next year to woo.

How can chickadees'
spare muscle and bone
sinew and feathers
withstand the cold of
northern winters?

I returned home in the evening and gave
In to the eventuality of
The season as there does come a point of
No return — in spite of my urge to save
Money — what I felt inside was a wave
Of chilly onslaught which I do not love
So I capitulated and I shoved
A little lever to become a slave
To the thermostat and to my furnace
Once again because I am not like my
Kitcat equipped with fur but am truly
A bare creature and my epidermis
Is prone to the shivers — though I may try
To deny it — the cold facts are ugly.

In Minnesota
the temperature is like
a toothache when at
a definite point we know
that things aren't getting better.

Sometimes I don't know why I bother to
Confabulate with words on paper when
I'm confused and don't know how to begin
But once I get going I do get clues
And the writing becomes a rendezvous
Of amusement and worthiness wherein
My words and humor become a linchpin
In revealing to me what I should do
Because things hold together — or they don't —
And I can waste my time asking "Why not?" —
Which I do regretfully — or I can
Simply experiment with words which can't
Hurt me while I frolic with verbal knots —
And I don't think half-rhyming is a sin.

I'm on a quest to
see how much nonsensical
verbiage I can
slather on a page before
you revolt and stop reading.

of

For some reason he chose the title "**of**"
And I don't know what he was thinking of
And perhaps it was because of his love
Of words that he selected a word of
Little significance almost drained of
Worth except to serve the language thereof
As it does so humbly play the role of
A connection between the words above
Its own articulated power of
Description as opposed to "Molotov
Cocktail" which are two exquisite words of
Incandescent quality with much of
The air of urban revolutions of
Fiery history you may have heard of.

My friend Cid Corman
wrote a two-volume set of
poems of over
1,000 pages with the
provocative title "**of**."

My Mom suffered a spasm of the neck
About a month ago and as she is
Eighty-six years old her condition was
Awful because for days she was a wreck
In terrible pain and we rushed to check
At the clinic with a doctor to quiz
Him about the trouble and to get his
Diagnosis/prognosis with the tech
Of ultra-modern pharmacopeia
And we got some pain-soothing medicine
But mostly our task was to provide care
As now we know there's no panacea
And it's helpful to have a regimen
Of watchful care in which we siblings share.

After a month Mom
is almost back to normal
except that she can't
turn her neck to the right and
so she's not able to drive.

I don't know whether she's my girlfriend or
Not but we've spent a lot of time with each
Other and I believe that she's a peach
And I'd really like to open the door
To a deeper relationship before
Something might happen and she's out of reach
And I aim to be playful in my speech
As I really don't want to be a bore
But I'm only meeting her once a week
Usually at a restaurant and
We talk for an hour on the phone at
Five a.m. and I've had more than a peek
Of her person which stimulates my glands —
I am what am and that's a tomcat.

I have the proclivity
And the creativity
To make her giggle
And then to wiggle
With just my verbosity.

It becomes obvious when a girl gets
Under my skin and starts to bother me
When I'm losing sleep and my thoughts aren't free
When I'm not with her and begin to fret
About her and it's difficult to let
Go and I feel my insecurity
And then I question my maturity
And a part of me certainly regrets
Becoming so damn dependent on her
But when I am with her I go out of
My way to make sure she has what she needs
And I'm shocked at what I do on the spur
Of the moment I think because of love
Which isn't gentle but does make me bleed.

When I'm with her in
a group of people whom I
don't know I don't give
a damn about what they think
and I'll look foolish for her.

This kind of love isn't gentle at all
I do regret my insecurity
I don't like manifesting jealousy
And there are days when I'm in a freefall
When I think that she could be my downfall
As she really appears to be carefree
While I don't know how she feels about me
And I get tired of the folderol
Because I suspect that she doesn't feel
Insecure like I do and she isn't
Losing sleep as I am because I do
Worry that loving isn't a big deal
For her and whether it is she doesn't
Show it — leaving me to simmer and stew.

But then there are times
when our words mesh together
so beautifully that
I am exuberant and
I forget all my troubles.

Of course I have to write about it as
I'm doing my gig of "everyday mind"
And I'm working hard at it — in a bind —
Scrounging for topics with razzamatazz
And love is material with pizzazz
And isn't infatuation defined
As what happens when poise is left behind
When I'm seized by unpredictable jazz
And as love has encumbered my life how
Could I have done anything else but
Grapple with it and put it on paper —
To admit that I may be crazy now —
And to make my insanity clear-cut —
Suggesting that love may be a vapor.

The object of my
love is a person with such
gravity that I
became a moon orbiting
her sunny brilliance.

—*Tekkan*

Book IV

Perhaps you haven't noticed yet but the
Mind is a wild epiphenomenon
That pops into existence carried on
From continuing vibrations of the
Tiny particles following on the
Cosmic cataclysm still going on
That we have named the "Big Bang" that brought on
Everything out of nothing which is a
Strange phenomenon that's hard to put one's
Finger on and appreciate — and then
You may not have noticed that you have no
Control of so many thoughts — which is fun —
When thoughts just pop into existence when
Least expected at a crazy tempo.

Can you say
what your next thought
will be — and how much
trouble it will cause?

I do scribble about "everyday mind"
Because it's a phenomenon that we
All share and is as simple as can be
And it's not at all difficult to find
But I wonder if I've clearly defined
It enough for you to see how easy
It is not to notice its repartee
For everything that happens is aligned
With "everyday mind" and everything in
The world wouldn't even exist without
Its presence and it's more than the ego
As its fine-woven roots are twined within
Cosmic significance despite self-doubt
As it is consciousness both high and low.

It is the unborn
and undying quality
of consciousness that
exists everyday along
with what is ephemeral.

One of my apple trees is losing its
Bark along its west-facing side and I've
Noticed the branches along the west side
Have been barren of leaves and how sad it
Is to observe my tree going to bits
And I suppose that it's destined to die
Perhaps because the summer was so dry
And there's nothing that I can do to fix
The situation — and I remember
Planting this apple tree because of its
Fruit and its blossoms twenty years ago
With my young family at the center
Of my life — and the tree is on the fritz
And the family dispersed a while ago.

I've adopted the
Japanese tendency
for tasting the sad
transitory nature of
life in the blossoming trees.

What would happen if the idea were
Taken seriously that the thing that
Happens suddenly and the person that
Responds are not separate things but are
Only one happening? Would it be far-
Fetched and such a distortion to look at
The doer and the deed as one thing at
The moment — and would you think that's bizarre?
A poem is happening now and words
Are rising to defined prominence from
A jumble of possible words that are
Subjective and would it be so absurd
To think the poet and the words that come
Reflect cosmic connection that's aware?

It's hard not to get
caught in the idea that
the doer makes it
happen and to minimize
what the cosmos is doing.

I've been exploring Agatha Christie
Paperback murder mysteries that are
On my Dad's bookshelves and the pages are
Yellow with age and I love the intrigue
And so I am reading without fatigue
Because the words that she has chosen are
Perfect for the people and times that are
Vanished now and her plots are so twisty
That I never know what's going to happen
And yesterday I saw on the cover
A fingerprint in what I recognized
As printer's ink and so I was saddened
To realize that my Dad had hovered
Over this novel and was mesmerized.

The printing press that
we both operated
became obsolete
and now the room is empty
except for the memories.

I am incurably curious and
Ask myself questions that I can't answer
And I think the cosmos is a dancer
With the earth spinning on its axis and
Orbiting the sun annually and
With the solar system moving faster
Orbiting the Milky Way — and it's queer
That the Milky Way is moving too and
Going even faster moving away
From wherever the Big Bang exploded —
And I want to face in each direction
One after another but I can't say
How to find each direction within mid-
Air — and these become perplexing questions.

At this moment I am
going in four directions
at the same time —
I want to *know*
the direction
of the earth's rotation
the earth's orbit
the solar system's orbit
and the direction
of the Milky Way.

I am conflicted when I gaze at my
Cottonwood on the corner of my yard
Because it continually bombards
The grass with twigs and branches and they lie
There until I pick them up and I sigh
Because it's troublesome and then it's hard
When all the leaves come down without regard
For my schedule which quickly goes awry
But then I see how fitting the bark is
With its deep grooves for the squirrels to grab
Ahold of and to climb and in winter
The tree's unsymmetrical beauty does
Seize my curiosity in the drab
And frigid season that makes me shiver.

The pure yellow of
the leaves in autumn reminds
me that in China
only the Emperor could
wear the color of the sun.

I am as puny as an army ant
And subject to superior power
Earth rotates at 1,000 miles per hour
I can expostulate and I can rant
But I'm not that much quicker than a plant
Earth orbits at 67,000 miles per hour
Maybe I am a walking sunflower
Unaware of gravitational slant
The solar system orbits the Milky
Way at 500,000 miles per hour
And the Milky Way is very weighty
Speeding at 1.3 million miles per hour
So I am barreling that fast too — *whoopee!*
I'm in the belly of cosmic power.

The speed of light is
186,000
miles per second —
is that quicker
than a thought?

Whenever I think about the future
It won't happen like I imagine it
So why worry even a little bit?
But I think I know what's going to occur
And I concoct my plans as I prefer
Manipulating for my benefit
Thinking of scenarios to outwit
Certain people who I want to deter
But with certain problems I do admit
I can't foresee the snares I will incur
With many outcomes that I won't permit
And I am careful but I only spur
Anxiety — which makes me a halfwit —
Whatever I do the future's a blur.

I'm very clever
and have my best interests
in mind so I am
prepared anticipating —
but it won't happen like that.

Rest in Peace Mike Finley

The sorrow of his daughter's death and the
Disappointments of his life tormented
Him but his misfortunes also sweetened
Him giving his curiosity a
Wicked edge and his vitality a
Biting restlessness which I think he used
To drive his intensity which deepened
Him and I guess that he always had a
Sharp and ridiculous kind of humor
But his suffering gave him sympathy
With the many friends whom he got to know
And as he was a great storyteller
I always noticed his sincerity
Which was a quality that made him grow.

He asked me if I
had children and I replied
that yes I did and
he sincerely suggested
that I simply just love them.

I'm at an age when it is typical
To have known many people who have died
And I think it's helped me to decide
How to be sensible and practical
And feel the emptiness of funerals
To sample the emotions that abide
After the ambitions are set aside
To face the fact of the unthinkable
And maybe my friends will die before me
And few will be left to remember me
Perhaps just several of my family
So it's better to drop my vanity
To be as genuine as I can be
And not be angry — and let things be.

My life will have been
mostly a success if at
my passing those who
know me remember my jokes
and I am not a burden.

At Aldi's grocery store the checkout
Clerks are inquisitive and they inquire
Whether I found the things that I require
And I politely say I've looked about
That I've been careful and hunted throughout
And though I did not tire or perspire
There is indeed something that I require —
I'm not irascible and I don't pout
But there's something to find out about as
I couldn't find my favorite zebra
Or the peppered hippopotamus so
I'm glad the clerk inquired of me and was
Hospitable because it's not the law
And their service is better than so-so.

These clerks don't know how
dangerous and inviting
it is to ask an
open-ended question to
a bored individual.

I am a blasé individual
And my job is to observe politics
To study all about their dirty tricks
And every day it is so typical —
Lying and cheating is continual —
I'd enjoy beating them with whips and sticks
As they're no better than blood-sucking ticks —
And I believe I am forgivable
When I am neglecting what I should do —
Instead of working I'm writing sonnets
Making fun of these political creeps —
If you were me wouldn't you do that too?
They think they're special with glamor and glitz
I've no idea of how they can sleep.

Sanctimony and
righteousness are oh so
propitious for
leveraging a useful
topical accusation.

I used to think that rhyming sonnets was
For the birds because it becomes a drag
And I don't want my poetry to sag
Into feckless stupidity because
I force words together and ignore flaws
While I simply enjoy creating gags
And I do admit that I like to brag
Which consecrating a new poem does
But you should picture me with a sly smile
As I imagine you reading my words
After all this is just mindless fooling
Which I could keep repeating by the mile
So don't blame me if you think it's absurd —
You see it's your time that I've been stealing.

Have you wondered what
the expression "for the birds"
actually means?
Does it imply something is
lofty or ridiculous?

Elliptical orbiting seems to be
A motion that the cosmos loves to do
As even the electrons do it too —
There is so much moving that we don't see
When the planets approach their apogee —
Solstice and equinoxes happen too
The cosmos is dancing a whoop-de-do
And I often forget to say *whoopee* —
But when I notice the sugar maples
That turn into the brightest of crimson
Yellow or orange I can't help but mark
The movement of seasons and I'm able
To cherish the quality of the sun
As the difference of the light is stark.

Scientists discovered
that quarks exhibit
either a left- or
right-handed spin.

Sonnets are a Houdini trick with words
Which I used to think was ridiculous
Because the rhyming is superfluous
Flimflam unless I want to be absurd
Turning rhyming couplets into passwords
So my poetry may be frivolous
Though my intentions are meticulous
But I won't let my essence become slurred
And I am writing sonnets because I
Fell in love with them while waiting for a
Train in Amsterdam while passing time with
Shakespeare's complaints about love and I try
To recapture youthful naiveté
By being a preposterous wordsmith.

I combine
sincerity with
play and confusion
circles into clarity.

Shakespeare lathered on the melodrama
Writing monuments of words about love
And such highfalutin fluff is above
My experience — which is of trauma —
So I'm expanding my panorama
By wanting a woman I'm unsure of
That perhaps I should be more careful of
Because in her own words she gave me a
Warning while we were driving together
The other day saying that the worst that
Could happen would be that we would split with
No further communication — and her
Offhanded comment may become a fact
Of life that I will have to contend with.

The bard wrote
140 sonnets
about an affair
offering no
resolution.

Foolish politicians are sometimes said
To have created circumstances by
Their wickedness wherein they have to lie
And keep on lying with increasing dread
Lest their true character be discovered
As the lust for power intensifies
The magnitude of deceit multiplies
And all they can do is to speed ahead
Deceiving themselves with everyone else
As if they are riding a tiger and
Holding on and being carried along
Lest they tumble off and meet the abyss
Of being eaten by the tiger and
That kind of justice is worthy of song.

Are my own
self-deceits
hypnotic illusions
and snares of love
like riding a tiger?

There was the day at the bagel shop where
I met her for breakfast when she saw a
Table of other guys and she said a
Few of them were datable if things were
Different and I suppose that she cares
About me but there was much more than a
Hint of indifference and maybe a
Dosage of cruelty inside of her
Words which was shocking — and on another
Day we arranged to meet again at the
Bagel place and I waited for her but
She didn't come and so I called her number
And she said she changed her plans without a
Reason — and I was upset — but so what?

Yeah! I think I've
written enough love sonnets
to have fulfilled the
tradition so now I'm free
to address other puzzles.

We don't use quill pens and ink and paper
Any more for the writing of poems
But we do have to have a stratagem
And mine is to stimulate a caper
To have fun and be critical later
By all means not to be *ad hominem*
Especially within a requiem
Where I would be an abominator
But it is my game to finagle words
And to fiddle with a catgut line of
Logic well enough to string a reader
Along skirting the edge of the absurd
Perhaps sprinkling a poem with love
Happy to be a communicator.

I would like to leave
readers with the impression
that I've given them a
a series of bonks on the
forehead with a feather.

Whatever there is to awaken to
The masters who have done it do say that
It can't be seized by force of will and that
There's absolutely nothing one can do
To manhandle its arrival and so
I am lost in a labyrinth of what
It means "to do nothing" to be poised at
A point that only breathing is what I do
And even that is doing something a bit
More than not doing anything as my
Mind is incubating a mess of thoughts
No matter how quietly I can sit
And I'm absorbing so much with my eyes
And with a line of geese I do get caught.

Liberation is
a puzzle as the masters
say the happening
is outside of traditions
and words cannot capture it.

There are so many things to think about
And most of them are just nagging details
As I would like to boost my monthly sales —
I'd like to have fame and money and clout —
Occasional loneliness makes me pout —
Could I be a sailor unfurling sails?
Could I satisfy myself spotting whales?
And how often would I spot a whale spout?
My energy goes into managing
My house and when there are unusual
Disturbances I have to check it out
And yesterday Kitcat was galloping
About and then I heard a strange jostle
And a tapping sound to find out about —
Curiosity is stimulating.

Kitcat jostled the
door from the inside of
the cupboard above
and behind the top of
the refrigerator.

He's a creature of curiosity
And I have underestimated him
Because he can be a creature of whim
Scampering in fits of velocity
Showing animal grandiosity
Which could imply that he's a little dim
But he's very clever with his forelimbs
And surprises me with dexterity
As every morning he waits for me to
Brush him and when I'm through I put the brush
On the floor and he seizes the brush and
Turns it upward and he endeavors to
Brush his furry face himself in a rush
And it's almost as if his paws were hands.

I thought that Kitcat
was only able to brush
one side of his face —
then I saw him turn about
and he brushed the other side!

It happened again at the grocery
Store that another checkout clerk inquired
If I had found the things that I required
And once again I said I didn't see
Just where the hippopotamus could be
And again I saw that I inspired
The disorientation I desired
Which I can use to write my poetry
And then I saw the previous girl and
I told her about my caper and asked
If she wanted to hear my poetry
About herself zebras and hippos and
She did and so we moved off to the side
Where I could become a luminary.

In a corner at
the front of Aldi's I
read my doggerel
about my earnest search for
zebras and peppered hippos.

The maple trees in Japan grow tiny
Leaves that turn a lovely shade of crimson
That I anticipated in autumn
And like the plum blossoms and cherry trees
They are celebrated by Japanese
And over the years I have taken on
Rituals and I am depending on
A mysterious sensibility
To mark the poignant unexplainable
Beauty blossoming and passing every
Season by writing poetry that shows
My appreciation for the maple
Trees that turn such lovely colors every
Autumn on the verge of winter shadows.

The *momiji* trees
are pronounced "momeegee" in
Japanese and once
one has seen them
one always remembers them.

I can't imagine William Wordsworth or
John Keats using the topics that I do
And also worthy Aristotle too
Would object and perhaps even abhor
The déclassé subjects that I adore
But I'm not a fool and I've thought it through
Because "everyday mind" is what I do
Which tells me there's no reason to be bored
With ordinary activity so
Three times a week I stand like a silver-
Back gorilla and heave a 100-
Pound dumbbell up and down and I can go
Very fast because I'm a believer
In exercise — and I'm not an egghead.

I am repeating
a pattern of lines and rhymes
that poets have used
for centuries for fun and
why not be innovative?

The clouds move at a gentle pace across
The sky and every season takes some time
To reach fruition and it's a pastime
Of mine to note the continual loss
Of the autumn leaves that I see are tossed
In the blusters of the wind and sometimes
They fall in batches and at other times
They waft and spiral by themselves and cross
My sight which I savor with a joyful
Melancholy — a sad festival — a
Month of dissolving when the leaves come down
And winter soon arrives and the cheerful
Leftover brilliance of the sun in the
Colors of the leaves lies drab on the ground.

Overcast days and
sharp winds howling through
the barren branches
have about them a bleak
and austere kind of beauty.

I do struggle to meet people where they
Are as I understand that they differ
From me as there are so many fissures
And difficulties getting in the way
Subtle and brutal leading us astray
As if differences were like scissors
Separating us as disbelievers
But we could talk on a happier day
As modern life in America is
Divided by ideological
Poison hyped by the mass broadcasting of
Continual accusation that does
Its best to foster pathological
Hatred — the polar opposite of love.

Differences of
race gender ethnicity
are so needlessly
exaggerated and are
slyly exacerbated.

I knew an intellectual guy who
Was an executive at a think tank
In Washington D.C. with so much swank
One had to have connections to get through
His layers of protection and I knew
Him partially and he wasn't a crank
And he well deserved the highest of ranks
Among thoughtful guys one could bump into
But only in his obituary
Did I discover his admiration
For hippopotami which he expressed
With all sorts of hippopotamus toys
And with obsessional jubilation
Which was not at all what I expected.

I can see that a
hippopotamus is an
ebullient mixture
of weighty pomposity
and impetuosity.

I don't mind being among people who
Have opinions and expectations that
Are opposed to mine but if they are at
Odds with me I'd like to be able to
Talk it through but so often now it's true
It's very difficult to arrive at
A place of neutral ground so to get at
The pivotal issues I look for clues
For flexibility grace and humor
Because I'd enjoy a healthy debate
And I am eager to learn something new
But political divisions are sour
And society is poisoned with hate
So being circumspect is what I do.

Being trapped in the
same room with my poetry
political and
Buddhist friends would become a
delicate balancing act.

If I were to say nothing sensible then I could
Avoid the trap of becoming preachy
And part of me thinks it would be peachy
To publish my books *without words* which would
Be a conundrum to my readers which could
Lead them to believe they were terribly
Cheated so I could be adorably
Quizzical and speculate that we should
Not play the game of believing that we
Ourselves are more tolerant and more
Broadminded than you other people are
As we wallow in our humility
But then I would risk becoming a bore
And whatever I say would seem bizarre.

An empty page
is empty of ideas
and flavorless.

Trimming about the rose bush I got a
Splinter imbedded in my thumb which I
Didn't notice while working to apply
The hedge cutter to daylilies and the
Hostas cluttering the yard which is a
Fall ritual wherein I bend my thighs
And spine to level the slicing blade by
The ground and then to rake and gather the
Leaves I straighten my back not noticing
The unusual strain on my body
And this year I could just pull on most of
The plants and they detached with my yanking
Which was easier than I thought it'd be —
To be done was what I was thinking of.

Leaves are in bags
a splinter's in my thumb
and I didn't notice pain
until I stood and walked.

My friend Jason the ecologist took
Issue with my saying that the trees are
Unsymmetrical pointing out that they're
More exquisitely balanced than they look
Otherwise they'd collapse when they are shook
By the wrenching of the winds and as far
As the spreading branches go they too are
Balanced by the displacement of their roots
So even though there's not a straight line or
A perfect curving form to be observed
There's a subtle composition of poise
Supporting every twist and crook before
The buds of the leaves are prepared to spread
In an epitome of equipoise.

The trees harmonize
with the rotation of the
earth synthesize
with the orbit of the earth
and with the strength of the sun.

Modern people are sophisticated
And with mathematically verified facts
We comprehend both galaxies and quarks
Our disproven theories are updated
Conflicting paradigms are debated
We measure our land with accurate maps
And with nanotechnology perhaps
Utopia is anticipated
While I'm watching the sun as it's rising
Doing my best to imagine that I
Can sense the movement of the earth
That I can feel the horizon moving
And can know the protection of the sky
As if this day were a glorious birth.

It's easier to
notice the pulsation of
my blood and heart and
the swelling the pause and the
dissipation of my breath.

On the corner of my property there
Stands a gargantuan cottonwood and
Now that I've disposed of the hostas and
Daylilies I have to wait and to bear
The dread of the labor to come — to fare
As well as I can — when I take in hand
My rake and lawn bags — when I stand and bend
Shoving the leaves into bags with the flair
That I'm accustomed to — but now I have
To watch and to wait as some of the leaves
Are the brightest of yellow and some are
Pristine green and it is tricky to stave
Off my dread as part of me really seethes —
Which I know to you may appear bizarre.

I bend over and
straighten up for many long
hours and afterward
for several days — because I'm
sore — I waddle like a duck.

Oh! what the tricky rosebush did to me
I thought that I had a thorn in my thumb
Though the day I got it my thumb was numb —
I do not indulge in hyperbole
What the rosebush did was a travesty —
I knew where my prickly thumb came from
I'm really quite clever — I am not dumb —
But I didn't see the reality
There wasn't only one thorn inside my
Thumb but three and so because my thumb was
Numb it took several days to see the truth
Whereupon I seized my tweezers to pry
Them out but I got only two because
Life is difficult — and also uncouth.

The leftover thorn
is there in the middle of
my thumb and I can't
retrieve it and it remains
a nasty provocation.

The leaves are descending gradually
And the forms of the trees are apparent
Their gesturing branches are transparent
The season displays a poignant irony
The way of the world is polarity
Summer days were sweltering — now they aren't —
Nothing upon the earth is permanent
Winter is a time of austerity
But how strange it is that before the leaves
Fall off they turn into the most brilliant
Of colors worthy of jubilation
Before the onset of a winter freeze
And to me the autumn leaves represent
A brief expression of exultation.

Who is it that cares
that everywhere on the
earth rainbow colors
will burst into expression
and then suddenly dissolve?

I thought that I was through with her and then
She called and apologized giving me
A story about being suddenly
Despondent and full of self-revulsion
And when that happens there's a compulsion
To sympathize with female company
She said and she called Donna and Sherry
And they went shopping and later on when
She realized that she left me hanging
Waiting for her she said she was sorry
And she wants me to forgive her again
As this is a time when she is hurting
And she's not angry at men — like Sherry —
And she knows that I understand her pain.

I marvel at how
she maneuvers me into
a position where
she neglects me and then she
plays upon my sympathy.

I haven't been angry with her after
All the things she's put me through — at least not
In her presence — but she's tied me in knots
Of frustration which I haven't shown her
And she's very difficult and she spurs
My perplexity now that I am caught
Between attraction and being distraught
Which I cannot let happen forever
Because I'm waking up in the middle
Of the night unable to quiet or
Divert my mind from her and getting up
Doing Zen still leaves me in a muddle
Which means that I have to do something or
Else go on being nervy and screwed up.

I had a taste of
being relieved of tension
and uncertainty
so maybe I can try some
purposeful indifference.

I can see how the monks of Asia would
Separate themselves from the tangles of
Ordinary life like romantic love
Because it's much easier and how could
One follow the allure of womanhood
And liberation also — so full of
Conflicting perplexities are both of
These paths — and yet I think it would be good
In each case if I could learn to relax
When I would like to — and when I need to —
Because so often my emotions run
Away with me inflicting painful cracks
In my composure and knowing what to
Do is easier when I'm having fun.

Surely with either
romantic connection
or a Buddha kind of
of liberation things would
come easier with a smile.

Rhyming sonnets is only a game that
I play and in choosing my words I make
A spontaneous bet and so I take
A real risk with my time and effort that
I can find a harmonious word that
Rhymes and that also pleases for the sake
Of rhythm and sense as it's a mistake
To focus narrowly and to fall flat
With the poem's overall impact as
Reciting a poem is like telling
A joke and if the punchline doesn't work
If there isn't any razzamatazz
And then if I look like a ding-a-ling
My handiwork fails — and I am a jerk.

There is such fun in
the spontaneity of
seizing on a word
and mixing it with other
words to make a quirky joke.

At the top of an ash tree I saw a
Couple of crows and the leaves were down at
The very top but were holding on at
The middle and the crows perched apart a
Little distance silently and then the
Crow on the right bobbed and cawed and then the
Other bobbed and cawed in a manner that
Suggested they were irritated at
Each other tangled in some sort of a
Disagreement and were sniping at one
Another in the way that couples do
And I thought what a dreary scene it is
And how powerful it is when one shuns
The other — and even animals do
It too — and how depressing it all is.

After a passage
of silence and sniping the crows
departed and flew —
together — leaving the tree
to shed its remaining leaves.

I am going on with the idea
That I have my sensual faculties
And my various attitudes and these
Are my determining phenomena
And — because of my dipsomania —
I believe that I can't do as I please
Can't indulge every urge that I am seized
By and if there is a panacea
It's what I can do with my attitude
And I realize I can't wrench myself
Into a better way of feeling but
That I can with a practiced latitude
Let go — as any emotion in itself
Is fleeting and need not become a rut.

If I'm able to
gently coexist with my
perplexities and
frustrations they will simply
dissolve — eventually.

Very often with groups I've been part of
It seems I'm on the outside looking in
And emotions arise that are akin
To aversion with the loneliness of
Being apart and with the confusion of
What to do to quell disruption within
That leads me to self-justification —
When what I want is acceptance and love —
But it does me no good to run away
From such puzzles and I think that it's good
Practice to see what happens over time
To discover whether there comes a way
For harmony to arise — so it would
Be best to be patient in the meantime.

I do have to live
with painful paradoxes
with abiding faith
that I don't have to impose
a forceful resolution.

You may have noticed that I am seeking
Enlightenment by writing poetry
Which maybe is conceited lunacy
As I'm taking pleasure in exploring
Sensuality and in detailing
Ordinary events with clarity
Fixing on the potentiality
That happenstance may be conspiring
With way-seeking mind and I admit I
Can't grasp liberation by force of will
And the harder I try the less likely
I am to succeed — but shouldn't I try
As there is a chance? And maybe I will
Grasp what can't be grasped — at least consciously.

I would like to be
surprised by events into
a revelation
so I'm patiently waiting
and expecting a surprise.

The great gift of Sunday is that I don't
Have to do anything that's scripted by
My livelihood and that I set aside
Regular exercise and I don't
Feel guilty about it because I won't
Let my morning relaxation go by
Without easeful meditation to ply
Thoughts to carefree exploration so it's
Propitious to sit and linger at
My keyboard looking outside the window
As I am fishing in the air for words
With open childlike expectation that
If I wait — even though I don't know how —
Cheerful exuberance comes with my words.

Once I've exhausted
my perceptive energy
my satisfaction
allows me to do household
chores with a happy éclat.

I could be expending effort building
An intellectual superstructure
Weaving philosophical contexture
With metaphorical might resembling
A Gothic cathedral of soaring
Thought anchoring objective conjecture
With flying buttresses as a lecture
Of perfectibility humoring
My conceit with a lofty angled vault
Raised above an expansive lonely nave
Exquisitely enlightened with stained glass
Consistently eliminating faults
Believing myself to be very brave
Becoming an intolerable ass.

I can't live without
a reliable point of
view and while it's good
to be consistent I know
my thoughts are perishable.

I don't have or want a publisher
As I am publishing my books online
And edit exhaustively every line
Rereading every page five times over
And I am determined to do over
Any defective poem taking time
Thinking that any mistake is a sign
Of carelessness and so I look over
My books when they arrive and yesterday
While flipping through the pages I noticed
That one poem was a line space too high
On the page and saw I was betrayed
With a slighting of my *magnum opus*
By a laxity that escaped my eye.

However much I
finagle whatever I
do there seems to come
a moment when a puncture
lets air out of my balloon.

I wonder if a repeated pattern
Of words for example rhyming sonnets
Has intrinsic value or whether it
Is just an ego-based foolish concern
As a sassy display of skill to turn
A phrase in any direction to fit
The predetermined form showing off wit
Which at bottom is about self-concern
But I get bored easily and don't want
To write about the same things over and
Over and to keep going I want to
Answer questions and I don't want to flaunt
Verbal dexterity uselessly and
There is always more exploring to do.

I want to bump up
against the vague edge of the
inexpressible
and for that I'm going to need
much verbal dexterity.

A group of us have come to Pioneer
Park for a gathering which overlooks
The river valley with the dawn in flux
With light on the verge ready to appear
As the beauty of the day is austere
As the season is approaching a crux
Growing colder and darker in redux
Of a seemingly barren season near
Again but we have a portable fire
And we each have a time to say our piece
About experience not feeling drear
In our hearts and our meeting does inspire
A satisfying talk that does bring peace
That gives to the season a certain cheer.

A guy lingers on
the edge of tears wanting
not to break down
talking about memories
of deer hunting with his dad.

When I meditate I make an oval
With the fingers of my hands which rest on
My lap and sometimes I will dwell upon
The oval of my hands as a focal
Point and as my body is immobile
My hands are an epiphenomenon
And my whole consciousness is resting on
The oval space within my hands and so all
My thoughts are arising within my hands
And I hold the force of my life the flow
Of my energy in my hands the fire
Of my attention rests in my hands and
The beating of my heart and the bellows
Of my breath feed the air to my bonfire.

When I finish with
meditation and I move
about doing my
business I have a buffer
between me and disturbance.

The cottonwood on the corner of my
Property is a power unmindful
Of my preferences and I am fretful
Of the coming cold and every year I
Do try to mulch or to bag the entire
Dispensation of all its leaves careful
To finish before the snow comes grateful
To have my yard looking tidy so I
Don't have to do an autumn chore in the
Spring so that I watch the days go by and
I see and wait for the yellow leaves to
Fall but there is nothing to do in the
Meantime but to quell my impatience and
Linger until the heaps of leaves accrue.

The yellow flags of
cottonwood leaves turn and
reflect leftover
summer sunshine and once they
go the landscape becomes drab.

The truck's engine is roaring up the hill
Filling the morning air with commotion
A consequence of its locomotion
And I appreciate it with good will
Admitting that it's giving me a thrill
Thinking about the driver's devotion
The selfless service of his emotion
His destination being the landfill
As the truck is serving society
By picking up and hauling away a
Week's accumulation of garbage
The effluvium of technology
As it is a necessary and a
Helpful ennobling kind of cartage.

Conversation with
the average garbage truck
driver would be
better than that of a
typical politician.

There is a bush still holding on to its
Leaves right next to Cub Foods where I hear a
Bevy of tiny birds engaged in a
Twittering fit that's not even a bit
Self-conscious as I approach and they get
Quiet as I stand — and then I go a
Little way away and wait — and then the
Racket starts again sounding like half-wit
Commentary — so once more I creep near
And quickly a silence ensues again
But soon there comes a sniping here and there
And I really do think the little dears
Are upset with me and are making it plain
They want privacy and don't want me here.

I think this is the
reincarnated spirit
of a gossip who's
been disembodied into
separated synapses.

I've been thinking about my dignity
Because it often is about the size
Of attendance and I want to apprise
Myself of the best time auspiciously
For me to kick the bucket skillfully
With consideration to maximize
My funeral and not to minimize
The recitation of the litany
Of my accomplishments and I'd like to
Be sure that the story of my travels
And of my publications is told and
I'd like people to have a clear-cut view
Of my selflessness and of the travails
Of my entire life that weren't bland.

Perhaps the crematory
Would be most laudatory
So fling my ashes
In ocean splashes
And be celebratory.

Of course there wouldn't be much benefit
To having a ceremony while not
Enjoying it so I've given some thought
To faking my death writing my obit
Hosting my funeral where I could sit
In disguise among the entire lot
Of my acquaintance to see how distraught
They were and I certainly do admit
That I'm being quite melodramatic
But I'm curious about what they would
Say about me and afterward I'd just
Remark that there was some kind of mistake
Or misunderstanding and then I could
Say the newspapers aren't worthy of trust.

It's not about vanity
Or about my sanity
I'm not bitter
I could live better —
Improve my humanity.

I like to capture the moments of change
In the seasons and the predominance
Of the bare branches — and the somnolence
Of the trees arriving again feels strange —
And the appearance of snow helps to gauge
The sudden shift before my consciousness
Adjusts — as it is the coincidence
Of my watchful and considerate age
That I notice when most of the trees are
Stark and the snow is coating the branches
For the first time this year — as I have seen
This sight under a white sky that is far
Above for decades and today it is
Clear the impact of the branches is keen.

Branches are so
weirdly
explosively
gesturing and yet
they are dormant.

I am like the barn owl gripping a branch
In the woods on the verge of the setting
Sun meditative freezing and hunkering
Down and I am summoning strength to stanch
My dreary thoughts that like an avalanche
Are oppressing and perpetuating
A sense of impending gloom including
A hint of doom — and as winter blanches
The color from the earth so does the cold
Stiffen and sober me reminding me
That there are seasons of difficulty
That I can bolster myself and be bold
And that poised relaxation is the key
To happiness amid austerity.

The barn owl grips a
branch in the gathering gloom
patiently waiting
in the circumference of the
forest for the time to pounce.

How often does it happen that as I'm
Typing poems looking out my window
Experimenting with snappy lingo
That a chickadee appears passing time
On the hedge outside looking like a mime
Of joy hopping and flitting even though
The air enveloping him is below
Zero and so he embodies a chime
With winter and one might even say that
He rhymes with the cold even though he is
The slightest of creatures composed only
Of bone sinew and muscle without fat
Epitomizing effervescent whiz
Gamboling with frolicsome energy.

If only I could
be as frolicsome and spry
as a chickadee
amid the gloom of winter
my thoughts would be whimsical.

Sooner or later I am going to stop
Because writing sonnets isn't easy
And I wouldn't say that I am lazy
But I do have to write my agitprop
As political hijinks are nonstop
The quality of my thoughts is hazy
I'm thinking in rhymes and that's just crazy
It is true that every rhyme is a prop
Which I hope really pops and doesn't flop
Which truthfully serves as a sop to my
Ego which plays and habitually
Mops my insecurity on the hop
With my lines of nonsense that do not lie
That may well approximate poetry.

I do need some scrutiny
Of my insecurity
Rhyming is crazy
And makes me lazy
I'd rather have sanity.

Relaxation is very important —
If I could do it when I needed to
There'd be little else that I'd have to do
As I wouldn't be pensive or mordant
All my afflictions would be impotent
Insecurity wouldn't stick like glue
And whatever comes I could see it through
I'd be decisive — not ambivalent —
I'd like to be wholehearted while letting
Go of results so I wouldn't worry
But I can't do that very well and so
Now I am wholeheartedly accepting
My unquenchable insecurity —
Trying to relax — so it doesn't grow.

I have to relax
with however much of my
insecurity
there is at the moment and
there's nothing else to do.

Did you ever make a hideous face
With friends as a child — just being funny?
Today is laughing and smiling easy?
We humans communicate face to face
We have ample ability to grace
Our friends with affectionate repartee
Swapping carefree facial hyperbole —
When quiet and attentive we can trace
Our subtle and unspoken emotions —
But in our workaday ways our faces
Are serious and absorbed in our chores
Cogitating on mundane commotion
As we focus on faraway places
And much too often we find ourselves bored.

Hollywood actors
simulate sincerity
with lip-trembling clues
with watery eyes
with verisimilitude.

A crocodile doesn't show emotion
A snake can slither but it doesn't smile
An ostrich can scamper for miles and miles
Inexpressive in its locomotion
There are countless beings in the ocean
And most don't bother to demonstrate bile
As they eat each other in mindless style
A dolphin can be joyous in motion
An octopus is capable of play
An elephant shows wisdom in its eyes
A dog can be a source of sympathy
My Kitcat is frolicsome every day
Some animals are smart — and they don't lie —
They do lovable reciprocity.

We humans are
dubiously gifted with
politicians who
can deceive and accuse
innocent people with ease.

A holy person is liable to
Befuddle a novice by presenting
An odd statement of a nagging puzzling
Nature which the novice is supposed to
Ponder wholeheartedly and to come to
Absorb lovingly each of the words taking
The surface meaning and meditating
Over a day with nothing else to do
And as the mind naturally leaps from
Thought to thought to thought the absurdity
Of the teacher's remark asserts itself —
The eccentricity of the words worms
Itself deeper with an uncertainty
Whether the meaning will resolve itself.

If you wear shoes
with rubber soles
the whole world will
be covered with
rubber.

I'm not certain that a single-pointed
Concentration is the object of the
Exercise and I do suspect that the
Guru would like his words to be sampled
Like the bouquet of a fine wine inhaled
And absorbed throughout the hours of a
Day without the distracting snares of the
Frenzied rush of business complicated
By pressing problems needing solutions
Maneuvering crazy-making pressures
Burdened with a need for accomplishment —
But the guru does create the suspicion
That all of his nonsensical measures
Are only producing befuddlement.

When a pickpocket
encounters a saint
his only concern
resides in the saint's
pockets.

I'm sorry — it is hard to focus right now
I will do my best but I'm distracted
My poetry is being impacted
I want to do two things at once somehow
And I can't do either well anyhow
My phone is busy and I'm affected
Which is a thing I haven't expected
It's a situation that I allow
As I'm sitting at my desk trying to
Write poetry while also texting with
Women on Match.com — so that I am
Looking at my phone expectantly to
Finagle my talents as a wordsmith
And my head resembles a traffic jam.

The pacing of texts
is different from woman
to woman and it's
tricky to fashion the best
angle of approach with each.

Kitcat and I have been housemates for a
While and we understand each other well
And I can say he primarily dwells
Upon satisfying his appetite with a
Customary schedule and at times in the
Day he climbs on top of a small step stool
In the kitchen endeavoring to tell
Me that he is anticipating a
Serving of delicious treats which I keep
In a bag on the kitchen counter and
Then he yowls to summon my attention
And I am indulgent — though I don't leap
To placate him — but I lollygag and
Saunter and bellow to create tension.

Usually three
times in a day we do
a lion taming
routine — but who is training
whom is problematical.

How can I put my face to its best use?
Do I practice gestures with a mirror?
Can I make my sincerity clearer?
Should cordial expression be profuse?
Would passionate exhibitions seduce?
Could humble self-abnegation endear?
How should my curiosity appear?
And does subtlety produce the most juice?
When I observe Hollywood performers do
Their renditions of situations
They don't overplay their faces because —
Of course — they're comely and they don't have to
Impose their feelings with declarations
When elegant subtlety earns applause.

Perhaps I'd be much
happier if I forget
what my face does
and if I attend to
whatever is happening.

The window in front of my desk looks east
And there are oak trees to the west across
The street and the oak leaves are being tossed
By a wind finally having been released
And the leaves are falling making a feast
Of dissipation and I feel a loss
And I'm thinking how I can put across
The sweetness of melancholy increased
By the pace of descending oak leaves in
The air and the many trees before my
Eyes are already bare and their branches
Are moving in the wind to underpin
A tactile sense of disappearance tied
To patient curiosity that lives.

Just a few wispy
clouds moving southward give the
sky a pace and
a direction at odds with the
blustery movement of trees.

Oh! What my round bootlaces did to me
I'd walk around and they would come untied
Which was a constant slighting of my pride
With a forced feeding of humility
An unwanted idiosyncrasy
When all I wanted to do was to stride
And there I was frustrated standing astride
Sloppy laces — oh what idiocy —
And I'd have to bend over again in
Public places and retie the laces
Which seemed such an act of futility
And I couldn't be walking about in
Winter blizzards taking angry paces
With my laces trailing me shamefully.

A friend advised that
I had only to take the
rabbit ears of my
usual knot and double
knot and since then I do.

Don't think about what happened yesterday
And don't worry much about tomorrow
Wouldn't you rather belittle sorrow
To free your energy and get away
There's no use in fabricating doomsday
Settle yourself — and become a flambeau
If you're despondent then learn the banjo
Even responsible adults can play
You can surf the waves of your emotions
And while resting you may linger and watch
Disturbance dissipating before you
As it's all vibrating ceaseless motion
And nothing has to matter very much —
You need not be a miserable stew.

If only I could
learn how to relax just
when I wanted or
needed to then I could be
a harmless peaceful hippie.

It's not the same piece of winter sky that
I'm seeing outside the window as I'm
Breathing oxygen produced just on time
For this moment now and it isn't that
I'm insensitive or asleep or that
I'm unappreciative that winter rhymes
Year after year and that the seasons chime
Day after day but it's elusive that
I'm looking at the same twisty bare trees
And the so familiar high overcast
Sky and it seems that I've been here before —
Weary — still not knowing how to appease
A dreary restlessness — and yet a vast
Impending liberation is in store.

Looking past the same
bare branches — I remember —
it's a different sky
today and liberation
could happen in a blink.

Isn't it hilarious that so much
Energy goes into persuading a
Person to love you and I think it's a
Possibility that there's overmuch
Love available but that it is such
An elusive thing depending on a
Spontaneous connection that is a
Gift and all I can do is be in touch
With what I think is happening — even
Though it's true that I don't know — and isn't
It curious to play the role of a
Lost and lonely soul who does believe in
Surprises and to be one who doesn't
Quit and who is ready to be gaga.

Wanting love can be
a kind of hunger and so
I try to be as
light as a feather waiting
patiently to give my gift.

The thing I have to wrap my head around
Is the thought *nobody cares* which is a
Slap to a person's confidence and a
Blow to the ego which becomes a wound
When life's troubles appear as a beat down
And it seems that I am up against a
Tide of difficulty and I need a
Power greater than myself to face down
An impending sense of isolation
Of meaningless emptiness that can so
Easily take over a person's thought —
I am grateful for my incarnation
And am strong enough to take many blows
As I practice watching my train of thought.

Then I suppose that
the emptiness from which
everybody comes
is an indestructible
and curious *no-body*.

There is satisfaction in doing things
That are practical and tangible that
Everyone can grasp ahold of and that
They can appreciate which also springs
From accumulated talents and brings
A level of commercial reward that
Pays for all the necessary things that
Fill a household and takes away the sting
Of having to work so hard and I am
Thinking of a mason who works with bricks
And stone who applies his patience and his
Strength — a worthy workman using his hands
As I am sure he has mastered many tricks
Of his trade of which he's truly a whiz.

For three hours I
assembled an essay but
accidentally
deleted it with one
stupid tap on a keyboard.

It's not solely caffeine in my coffee
That I use to my advantage — and I'm
Sure the caffeine helps — but I know the time
Of the day when I have felicity
And I am most awake and it's easy
Then to connect my thoughts with words that rhyme
And then my emotions and grammar chime
Just when I'm having the most clarity
Because for most of the day I do my
Business on my own without the chance to
Use my words while I believe that life is
Best with conversation and I scrape by
Alone — as well as I might — but I do
Want to see what communication does.

I leverage
rhythmic energy
to communicate
with you who are
an open white page.

It's easy to blame politicians for
The screwed-up state of our society
As they take on responsibility
By simulating a show of candor
Knowing as they do it's hard to keep score
Of distant laggardly bureaucracy
Which creates societal entropy
While we citizens expect so much more
From our public servants and we tend to
Choose the politicians who are smooth at
Telling lies while we neglect to admit
That we would like to profit from a slew
Of subsidized government programs that
Can't last forever — as there are limits.

Those who exercise
power profit from
power — everyone
else squabbles over
scraps.

Do you suppose that he was serious
When he wrote those dozens of besotted
Sonnets in iambic bebop trotted
About as if he were delirious
With love which would be deleterious
To balance to be so tightly knotted
In confusion and to be so clotted
With passion appearing imperious
In one poem and then melancholic
In the next and isn't it curious
That he doesn't portray his lover with
Defined clarity which is symbolic
Of a fantasy and injurious
To the health of such an addled wordsmith.

Shakespeare's sonnets
are like the skull of Yorick
that Hamlet dug up
from the dirt — who can gauge
the jester's sincerity?

You know these sonnets are a fabrication
They're written in the spirit of a game
They're phantasmagoria without shame
As I am giving vent to my fixations
Where I can practice painless flirtations
Whereas real emotions can be a drain
And I would much rather play with the flame
Of a curious elucidation
And you may see each poem as a wall
Of words fitted tightly together like
The stones of Machu Picchu without
Mortar — or perhaps like the overall
Effect of a prosaic concrete dike
That says to a sea of boredom — keep out!

On every page of
this book there is a wall of
words wherein each word
does righteous duty without
any superfluity.

What does the whiteness of a page mean to
You as you turn the pages with the tips of
Your fingers as white is a color of
Purity and of being unsoiled to
The touch of the eye being easy to
Overlook as the words get the best of
Your attention and as the focus of
Curiosity the words proclaim to
You what is worthy of notice — but don't
Discount the quiet presence of paper
Sliced and so precisely weighted for the
Fingertips of readers because you don't
Recognize truth without the paper
Which is invisible — like the word "the".

Feathery clouds and
a new-fallen snow have a
soothing quality
so easy to overlook
against the pepper of life.

You have a story to tell and maybe
Your happiness comes in conversation
In simple and unhindered discussion
As the weight of experience is freed
And communication dispenses seeds
Of peace as you may escape delusions
Of all your self-punishing conclusions
As another person could set you free
With a healing of intimacy that
Dispenses with the need for caution as
There are people who can't be trusted but
Some of us are compatible with what
Feels so much like a hole in you and is
The burning of emptiness in the gut.

In my youth I met
a derelict old drunk who
asked me to write his
life's story but I didn't
have the energy for it.

For most people the holiday season —
Including Thanksgiving — is a time for
The gathering of family and for
The sharing of experience upon
The hardships that we don't have to dwell on
The getting over of life-numbing chores
And we have the chance to open the doors
Of our hearts to each other again on
Christmas and New Year's Day but for some of
Us there's a paradox of convention
That societal expectation makes
The spontaneous act of showing love
A difficult role that's full of tension
Inspiring a taste of sour grapes.

I'm grateful for the
Grinch who steals Christmas
for the elucidation
of the stubbornness
of the suffering.

There are deserts to cross on the way to
Liberation with the aspiration
With the impatience of expectation
That with mighty efforts I can accrue
The wisdom beyond wisdom and I do
The prescribed remedies for deflation
And I don't shirk my share of frustrations
And I have the resolve to see it through
Encountering the aftermath of the
Dissolution of my family that
Left me with a household full of items
Belonging to an ex-wife a son a
Daughter of trivial little things that
Bite me — what am I going to do with them?

I'm not ready for
the inspiration
of the memories
involved with every
trivial item.

An elephant is a ponderous brute
With provocative and curious eyes
It may be an impish elf in disguise
And it possesses a dexterous snoot
Which is a delicately touching snout
It makes use of its trunk to tantalize
To touch and caress and to socialize
And having such a limb must be a hoot
The elephant lumbers upon the earth
Its legs are like tree trunks with big round feet
Every footfall thuds and reverberates
Each echoing impact comes from its girth
It parades about in tuneful rhythm
Pounding about in a procession of beats
With thumping plopping steps that resonate.

The elephant can
hear the whopping of distant
elephants with the
sensitivity of its
attentive listening feet.

What would I do with an elephant's snout?
Could I turn the pages and read a book?
Or slice an onion with a knife and cook?
And turn a doorknob to get in and out?
And use a steering wheel to drive about?
Could I enclose a tulip's stem and pluck
Would I sniff a Coca-Cola and suck?
I'd swing it about if I were a lout
And could my elephant's appurtenance
Be an instrument of intimacy
Delicate enough to undo buttons
To unfasten bras with a nonchalance
To fondle soft breasts with intricacy
To probe inside of a bellybutton?

I guess the question
would revolve about whether
an elephant's trunk
would appear an enchanting
appendage on Match.com.

Every being possesses dignity
And I'm thinking of the worthy giraffe
Now you may be tempted to scoff and laugh
And read these lines for cheap hilarity
Which only shows your own barbarity
I am writing on the giraffe's behalf
And it deserves a witty epigraph
As it is an intriguing panoply
Giraffes don't care about your opinion
Giraffes embody elongated grace
Giraffes demonstrate curious caution
Giraffes exert a peaceful dominion
A giraffe has a respectable face
A giraffe is levity in motion.

To watch a giraffe
gallop over distance is
to see a loping
and a swinging grace that makes
locomotion beautiful.

It is not the most remarkable thing
About a giraffe and it looks puny
And it does appear a little loony
And if it chooses the giraffe could fling
It left and then if so inclined could zing
It right and when the giraffe is gloomy
It droops and when the giraffe is sunny
It swings and we could even say it sings
With happiness but it has prosaic
Use as the giraffe is assailed by flies
That tickle and bite the poor giraffe's rump
And there it is available to flick
The pesky flies before they even try
To bite — so the giraffe is not a grump.

The giraffe's plumy
tail appears exceedingly
laughable until
one sees it flick flies over
most of the giraffe's body.

He showers when he gets home at night so
He's free in the morning to wake and get
Out the door and he doesn't shave and lets
A week's worth of stubble grow and he goes
To work composed and I really don't know
How he can move without coffee and yet
That is what he does and he doesn't fret
Very much in his work-a-day tempo
Because he's done all the aspects of the
Job being a surveyor measuring
Distances and establishing order
About himself plotting points upon a
Grid and there's an ease in calculating
Numbers with no messes to get over.

If only people
in his life were as easy
to finagle as
numbers he wouldn't have to
grow loving roots into God.

I am attached to my morning shower
There are chores that I do before it
When waking I am only a halfwit
The minutes go by and I gain power
My brain gets going and my thoughts flower
Kitcat's hungry so I give him tidbits
I watch him run about — he doesn't quit —
When I don't feed him he does get sour
I traipse about the house for half an hour
Replenishing Kitcat's water and food
Taking care of his basement litter box
I read yesterday's poems and scour
Them for mistakes — I like my solitude —
My home resembles a childhood sandbox.

By the time I
enter the shower and
savor warm water
enveloping me my thoughts
are popping like popcorn.

Do you suffer from an attachment to
Your face being ever mindful of your
Appearance thinking it is a fixture
Of who you are that sticks to you like glue?
You can't escape no matter what you do —
And you do your best to create allure
To be genuine — but you are unsure —
Is your face only something you look through?
Is it even possible to think of
Who you are besides what you look like and
Can you imagine how differently
You would live without the idea of
Your appearance as if it were a brand
Which compromises elasticity?

How many hours
could you get by without a
mirror to make the
readjustments that you know
are absolutely needed?

We gather in libraries to read our
Poetry to each other handing out
Our poems and then we dangle our snouts
Over the pages to fuss and scour
Our verses trying not to be sour
Aiming to be helpful and not to spout
Piffle but to summon our best to sprout
Our creativity and to flower
In whichever way we choose to express
Because we want to use our freedom to
Say anything that we are moved to say
But how can we do that without finesse?
And I tend to be blind to my miscues
And it takes scrutiny to make headway.

Writing poetry
is like launching into an
acrobatic leap
and a writers' group performs
the job of a safety net.

I know I'm asking for trouble when I
Start reading profiles again but either
I act doing my best to be eager
Or I admit that I am too damn shy
And it's true that I'm not a quitting guy
So the goal becomes to be a seeker
While being mindful of my demeanor
But often all I can do is to sigh
While looking at girls on a dating app
Because no matter what I do it's so
That most of them don't bother to reply —
Yes — I know that is better than a slap
But I have to practice not feeling low —
It seems that the rules of hunting apply.

The object is not
to collect a harem but
to find one woman
who matches me well enough
to be a cozy couple.

There is quizzical Debbie to ponder
And she is not the one who is confused
But what she is doing has me bemused
She is a beauty which I can't ignore
With a sense of humor that I adore
My interest in her is already fused
But she leaves me feeling a little bruised
I can't determine what she has in store
She replies intermittently leaving
Me to dangle in between messages
Encouraging me by giving me her
Phone number but it is confusing
When I rouse myself and call she teases
By not answering — what should I infer?

She's agreed to meet
at India Palace after
the holidays which
is almost a month away
and does keep me lingering.

Sundays are my sanctuary when I
Can leave my bed at my leisure
And devote myself to mindful pleasure
Not having a work schedule to go by
When the heft of my business applies
I get to explore internal treasure
To plumb awareness and take my measure
And I am happy with what I come by
As I plant my bottom in my chair and
Fish for ideas in the air with the
View of my window — and every
Day mind is the game that I take in hand
And I know most of you would say — huh? —
Writing poetry is my reverie.

I am blessed by the
discovery that I can
lighten my mood by
playing with words and it's
fine being solitary.

I can imagine what it would be like
Having a girlfriend and devoting time
Nurturing each other trying to chime
Our emotions — and would I have to strike
A precarious balance not to spike
My poetry jazzing time? When I rhyme?
Could I be a boyfriend only part-time?
And I do hope that we could think alike
And give each other some necessary
Freedom because I can't imagine how
I could write with someone tapping or stomping
A foot behind me quite impatiently
With a furrowed forehead and angry brows
Devouring glowering souring.

Because once I sit
my rump in my chair time goes
by and I lose track
until it's late afternoon
and I've blown my energy.

The presence of the winter cold again
Can be a pleasurable sensation
A dash of bracing invigoration
It is a dance up to the edge of pain
And to partake of the season is sane
Winter can bring a touch of elation
One might even say it's a flirtation
With danger and I'm not one to complain
Except that I'd rather not meet winter
In my living room when my furnace stops
Working and I shiver trying to sleep
In a frosty bed and my breath appears
As ghostly vapor and I have to drop
Everything to fix it — I can't be cheap.

A fan went out in
my furnace and it cost me
$500
to fix it but winter was
banished from my living room.

I pine for female companionship but
Through painful experience I know by
Now that it does me no good to deny
The subtle hesitations of my gut
And to allow myself easy shortcuts —
Women say what they want and I comply
I am straightforward and I do not lie
And I guess it takes patience to abut
Myself with just the right woman who would
Appreciate me for who I am and whom
I could understand well enough without
Our having to argue and so we could
Grace each other and so we could assume
Love — without having to figure it out.

In America
I am wandering about
looking for a piece
of a scattered puzzle that
abuts on me perfectly.

How often do you look at things about
You before you stop noticing them as I
Am thinking of a sign that almost cries
"*Turn Off the Coffee Pot!*" which loses clout
Over time and so it does come about
That we do forget and afterward sigh
Because we don't remember — though we try —
We are not negligent — we are not louts —
The sign is something we don't think about
So the coffee burns into a hard crust
And has to be soaked chipped and then scoured —
Burnt coffee is difficult to get out —
The people at the church have lost their trust
It's true I think they have somewhat soured.

I think it's not a
bad idea to have on
hand a supply
of the glass pots easy to
dispose of from time to time.

The snow is falling in a steady pace
It is falling amid the homes and trees
Barren branches are swaying in a breeze
It is the morning but there's not a trace
Of the sun — the light is dim in this place
I am typing carefully on the keys
At the window watching snow at my ease
And I think the season is full of grace
Even as the color is erased from
The earth and there is no demarcation
Between the descending snow and the sky
And the scene will be dark for months to come
As this is the time for hibernation —
December is opposite from July.

This white paper page
represents new-fallen snow
and the ordered rows
of black letters on the page
stand for the barren branches.

The sun isn't visible so often
During winter and yet by mid-morning
The landscape is lighted — trees are moving
In the wind and the blusters aren't softened
By a touch of warmth and days are often
Devoid of obvious cheer and feeling
More than a little forbidding blending
Together over time and not softened
By the lively variety of growth
And yet the sun isn't really absent
And sometimes it appears as a shiny
Spot and — yes — the sky and sun are both
White — but the sun is certainly present
And it will be bright eventually.

Even behind clouds
the sun is incandescent
radiating heat
in every direction and
lighting a chilly day.

—*Tekkan*

Book V

The mechanism of a furnace lies
Outside the sphere of my understanding
And mine is especially frustrating
Involving a magnitude of surprise
That it burns fuel oil and most of the guys
Who fix furnaces are discouraging
And my situation is perplexing
As the bulk of the profession applies
Itself only to gas furnaces but
With the use of my determination
I found a couple companies who work
With oil and though there wasn't a shortcut
I did experience a redemption
By utilizing an expert's artwork.

Charles is a wealth of
genial information
and he replaced a
fan and tuned my furnace and
now it hums musically.

The utterances of crows convey a
Conspicuous thrust of intelligence
Expressed insistently with emphasis
And it's tricky to know how much of a
Range of meaning is involved or of the
Sort of feelings — maybe not gentleness
And perhaps there isn't much eloquence —
And whatever they're expressing there's a
Guttural ruthlessness that seems to be
In play that implies that there's a pecking
Order within a tribal dynamic
And when I see them gather in a tree
I can't help but wonder what they're saying
And whether I could be sympathetic.

To hear a single
crow caw on a cold morning
and be answered by
another in the same tree
is to hear a weird language.

In January in Minnesota
The landscape is buried in heaps of snow
The dark and cold are a dreary combo
Any skin exposed to the wind feels raw
We patiently wait for happenstance thaws
The passage of time is terribly slow
So I look to upturn the status quo
And provide myself a touch of hoopla
By picturing exotic flamingos
They are visions of loveliness in pink
Their curving necks appear like question marks
They help me to forget my frozen toes
Flamingos live in paradise I think
The contrast with Minnesota is stark.

It doesn't quite work
to escape Minnesota
by seeing happenstance
plastic flamingos encased
in a landscape of piled snow.

My reliable buddy is Kitcat
He reminds me of a mountain lion
No — he doesn't share the same kind of brawn —
He pounces and wrestles with the doormat
I feed him so well he's a little fat
He stretches in the sun and also yawns
Mostly it's houseflies that he preys upon
He springs and lunges like an acrobat
And Kitcat possesses a cougar's eyes
That appear quite dangerous when he stares
He saunters about with aggressive grace
Like a predator — but only pint-sized —
The house is encumbered with tawny hair
I like to seize his head and stretch his face.

I don't suppose a
mountain lion would allow me
to pin back his ears
and stretch out his entire
face — but Kitcat doesn't mind.

I rest the palm of a hand on his head
And pull both of his ears backward gently
Which is just my way of being friendly
And I see that his mouth begins to spread
Into a wide smile which could be misread
As goofy — his eyes are bulging widely
As I stretch — I'm tugging only slightly —
Kitcat is composed as he looks ahead
And from his calm demeanor I can tell
That he is happy lying next to me
On the couch — I stop pulling his face and
Push his ears down instead as we both dwell
In my living room watching the T.V. —
I pat the top of his head with my hand.

I can't imagine
other animals or
people letting me
play with their faces and ears
except for happy Kitcat.

The oak the ash and the maple on the
Shelf of a limestone bluff that looks over
The river valley are sights that confer
Quiet familiarity on a
Cold morning as we gather around a
Fire inside a portable container
And we do enjoy gazing at the fire
And we take such pleasure in watching the
Horizon brighten as the sun is rising
Up but hasn't yet crested — as we meet
Again for our talk — which may be crazy —
But we gather such strength by exchanging
Simple and honest words that help defeat
Fear and isolation — we aren't lazy.

After a person
has been sober for a while
alcoholism
becomes an afterthought — we
come for the conversation.

The flamingos aren't separate from the
Tropics the water and the algae that
They feed on and if they didn't eat that
Type of algae then they wouldn't be the
Curiosity that they are and the
Epitome of exotica that
I love to think about while knowing that
They are that pigment pink because of the
Algae they consume just as their very
Odd yet graceful necks and their spindly stick
Legs are at one with the temperate air
And with the shallows of the lakes and seas
Where they live — and it really is a trick
Of nature to appreciate and share.

North America
creates bald eagles finches
crows pileated
woodpeckers in addition
to pink plastic flamingos.

A box in my living room stopped working
A week ago so I wasn't able
To fixate on my favorite cable
T.V. shows and I know when I'm watching
That I am wasting my time absorbing
Toxic news that is unbelievable
With murders that are inconceivable
And so for a week I was relaxing
And dwelling within the quiet of my
Home lounging about with serenity
Separated from the cultural trash
Liberated from political lies
Free of the scripted personalities
Living without American mishmash.

A techie replaced
the broken cable box — and
television is
not as bad as alcohol
or cigarettes I suppose.

I look at the way that Kitcat saunters
In the living room when he pounces on
A pitiful mouse when he sets upon
A fly in the air and when he wanders
Through the house I think he is a wonder
Of physicality of predation
As he attacks without hesitation
And he is such a natural fighter
Then I think about a mountain lion
Wandering the highlands in winter
Hunting deer rabbit elk sheep or raccoon
As it saunters and alerts and lies in
Wait before it pounces — mad with hunger —
Wayfaring under the light of the moon.

He is not hungry and
is under no compulsion
to wander and hunt
and yet Kitcat is alive
at night — and rushes about.

Greetings to the sun — the maker of days
No stigma of waywardness touches you
Your fire is good mighty and ever new
You hold the life of each season in sway
Not for an instant is the earth astray
You are a sparkle in a drop of dew
You are reflective off the oceans too
You are the pivot of our life today
We owe our beating hearts and breath to you
You are what makes the colors visible
Yours is the light that illumines the moon
Every single tree reaches up to you
Your radiation is reliable
We mark a daily pinnacle at noon.

You are a balance of
crushing gravity and
gaseous combustion
that does inspire
imagination.

However fierce a mountain lion is
It doesn't carry anger in its heart
Surely it can rip a body apart
Watching stalking and waiting when it does
Tearing ripping and biting as it does
It's doing no more than playing its part
Performing a role that nature imparts
But it doesn't suffer self-hypnosis
We are people who aren't hunting our prey
We visit delis and supermarkets
We are organized efficient killers
Some of us aspire to be gourmets
As predators we are the exorbitant
But see how many suffer from anger.

An angry heart can
claw and rip and tear and bite
a human body
apart — all needlessly so —
from delusional motives.

Humans are prone to intoxication
Dominance is a brutal elixir
We say we want to make the world better
We have experts who provide prescriptions
Bureaucracies dispense instructions
Politicians lionize go-getters
Our systems are always getting smarter
We pride ourselves on robust production
But with persistance and careful awareness
It becomes obvious over time that
So much of what our leaders do turns out
To be deceitful and quite egregious
And then we can see it's apparent that
Society promotes dishonest louts.

Cynicism's not
healthy and compassion and
self-forgetting love
are real human virtues —
but don't trust politicians.

The idea of the sun is tricky
Without eyes I wouldn't recognize it
And without skin I couldn't caress it
I am grateful to be able to see
To appreciate what it means to be
It is easy to be a hypocrite
To believe in things that are counterfeit
Even my own opinions disagree
I do misunderstand reality
I give them no thought — yet my heart pulsates
And my chest swells and it empties of breath
There's grace and rhythm in simplicity
And endless confusion inside debates
Is consciousness really curtailed by death?

The sun exists in
the sparking of synapses
and in optic nerves
and the sun also orbits
inside of the Milky Way.

Outside the window and down a small hill
There's a white wooden fence that I can see
At one of its corners there is a tree
The fence doesn't move — it only stands still
Watching everyday there aren't many thrills
But every yard contains a panoply
Which is a sampling of reality
It is another quiet day until
A squirrel is scampering atop the fence
The fence is curving and goes up and down
The squirrel goes up and down and along
This is an ordinary happenstance
The squirrel likes the fence to get around
I think this sight is worth a little song.

When it gets to the
corner the squirrel jumps and
precariously
seizes ahold of a twig
and pulls itself to safety.

George Oppen is a poet I admire
He wrote a book — *On Being Numerous*
I think his book is sadly humorous
It's about the isolation we share
Of the desperation behind our stares
And of the cruelty that shatters us
Harrowing nightmares that we don't discuss
Of nagging thoughts that our lives are haywire —
There is a brick that the eye picks in a
Wall of bricks so quiet of a Sunday
That was waiting for you here Mary-Anne
He writes thinking of clarity in a
Sense of transparency — he doesn't say
What it means — he doesn't say that he can.

There is clarity
And transparency
silent clarity
but George doesn't mean
much can be explained.

If you'd like to escape the madness of
Our time you should read the *Ramayana*
A creation myth of the Brahmana
There are many ideals it speaks of
Such as ethics and loyalty and love
It's the heroic journey of Rama
Who kills the king of demons — Ravana —
Valmiki wrote characters whom I love
Such as Hanuman who is a monkey
He's the son of Vishnu the god of wind
He's a spy who leaps over an ocean
Hanuman is honored for loyalty
He's impetuous generous and kind
An avatar of divine emotion.

Ravana has ten
heads and twenty arms — he steals
Rama's wife Sita
and Rama leads an army
of bears apes and monkeys.

Thomas is a little blue tank engine
Percy's even smaller and he is green
And they are buddies on the railroad team
Then Bill and Ben are mischievous twins
James is brilliant scarlet and he is vain
Diesel is nasty holds grudges and schemes
Gordon's dynamic and really blows steam
When Thomas fouls up he feels such chagrin
These are the engines on "Thomas and Friends"
A children's show of a T.V. series
That my kids watched growing up in Japan
A childhood fantasy of odds and ends
Mornings were noisy with cheerful stories
Thomas is boisterous and I'm a fan.

Inside a small room
in the middle of a
little drab rowhouse
was a scene of tooting
and puffing tomfoolery.

I drove a scooter searching in Kyoto
I wore a poncho in summer showers
And a thick leather jacket in winter
There were many days when I would just go
I was a youthful roving dynamo
I visited each of Kyoto's toy stores
Hungrily seeking Thomas characters
I wanted them all and couldn't let go
Trevor the tractor was hardest to find
I hunted for him for two dreary years
I tramped department stores in rubber boots
The elusive tractor disturbed my mind
I was an adult — I didn't shed tears —
There did come a day when I found my loot.

Thirty years later
all the Thomas characters
are in a box in
my basement forgotten by
Joshua and Jocelyn.

I loved a dancer when I was twenty
I wrote a sonnet that I was proud of
About a candle innocence and love
When dancing nude she fascinated me
Ragged desire wouldn't let me be
Who cares that most people would disapprove?
Young and rootless — I had nothing to lose
I was empty innocent and naïve
I wrote lines while riding city buses
It's a pity that I couldn't know her
It was imagination that I loved
Daydreaming of kisses and caresses
She lives in me — a make-believe lover —
I do remember her when I am bored.

I translated her
womanly beauty into
adoring words that
embody a longing that's
still fresh through many decades.

I live in a house on a quiet street
It's a pleasure to hear the wind and chimes
I'd say their notes do variously rhyme
In boisterous blusters they sound offbeat
However they jangle they are upbeat
Perhaps the wind is a musical mime
The play of the notes is a pantomime
The daily performance is very sweet
I do often wonder what makes the sound
Is it the chimes or the breezes that sing?
On occasion the chimes will clang in wind
The wind strikes the tubes and vibrates around
I think that the vibrating air has wings
The song of chimes arises in my mind.

Without vibrating
air there isn't stimulus
without listening
ears and an open mind there
isn't reverberation.

Everything around us comes from the earth
Earth is below and also above us
Earth is about and even inside us
The wind the seas the sky come from the earth
The water in our cells comes from the earth
Its teeming biology nurtures us
Its mineral chemistry supports us
Bodily elements come from the earth
We can feel the earth is truly alive
We are its breathing manifestations
Do we understand it sufficiently?
Without its workings we couldn't survive
We are infused with its fluctuations
May we feel it and tread differently.

We and the earth are
not separate entities
we didn't come from
elsewhere — we aren't others —
but we are one and the same.

I'm not doing what I'm supposed to do
That is what the critic inside me thinks
A punishing impulse that becomes a jinx
There's the daily news to drag myself through
Crafting opinions is what I should do
Smartly addressing society's kinks
Absorbing data establishing links
Confabulating solutions on cue
There are factions of ideology
Systems of thought dividing our people
Strong emotions that are based on belief
Inspiring endless pathology
Creating a cancer — eating people —
What can be written to foster relief?

To argue over
the lies and oppressions of
the use of power
is an endless ambition
summoning pitiless words.

I think there is always liberation
To be found in relaxation and if
I can manage to relax even if
I'm having discouraging emotion
And feeling an impulse of aggression
I could lift the weight from my shoulders if
I pay attention to my breathing if
I let go of endless complication
As I always have the luxury and
Leisure of drawing oxygen into
My lungs and I can close my eyes also
And with every breath there is peace at hand
There is nothing more that I have to do
I can surrender thought — and just be slow.

Outside the window
on the hedge chickadees
hop turn and flit off.

It's not so easy to imagine it
What would the earth be like without people?
In our absence would the planet be dull?
The life of the species would be well-knit
Cattle and chickens could relax a bit
The shores of oceans would host the seagulls
Their plaintive calls would remain an earful
But there wouldn't be humans to hear it
We impose self-consciousness on the earth
We dominate and rearrange nature
We argue and fight and make decisions
It is to the earth that we owe our birth
Insanity is part of our nature
Compounded with intelligent vision.

The cosmos birthed
restless and dissatisfied
self-consciousness and
even distant galaxies
may be encompassed.

Does the universe use my eyes to see?
I loiter at my desk and play with words
I gaze outside and encircle the birds
Does cosmic consciousness encompass me?
What is the impact of society?
Mass emotions are so often absurd
The result of adversity is blurred
What is the meaning of being empty?
I take such comfort in a vast blue sky
The moon's a homely companion at night
Thought of light years is disorienting
What good does it do to tell myself lies?
Bantering stories is my heart's delight
Breathing wholeheartedly is relaxing.

I am not and could
never be isolated
and alone within
these interpenetrating
haunting beautiful questions.

My poetry is a sunrise diary
I look for treasure in each of my days
Whatever life presents is A-OK
There are times of creeping anxiety
When I seek for balancing clarity
It's healthy to juggle with words and play
Pretending to host an *auto-da-fé*
There's irony in mock calamity
Every day has its own peculiar touch
I'd like to capture transience on paper
I want to communicate life to you
It's better not to expect very much
This is only glorified notepaper
A rhyming propitious whoop-de-do.

I scribble every
morning as the sun rises
and a bald eagle
just adjusted its wings in
a turn over the maple.

Hints of the poem are in the first line
Fresh is the snowfall that came overnight
Bright is the sunshine that helps me to write
Blind is the heart that is adamantine
I play with words and nonsensical rhymes
The pith of thought is depressingly trite
The weight of these words is gossamer light
I sit in a chair and while away time
Confabulate rhythm — forget the sense
Accumulate questions — abandon force
Approximate wisdom — don't try too hard
This poem is worth a couple of cents
These lines are obvious and are not coarse
My poem is lazy but it's not a canard.

I'm only playing
games today and I'm hoping
you're not serious —
the hair of my mustache
and on my chin became white.

She is a woman who stimulates seeds
She's a ragamuffin angelic girl
She has a head of thick natural curls
It's hard to know where attraction will lead
Longing is wretched and has made me bleed
I see my thoughts are beginning to swirl
I want to avoid a compulsive whorl
How can I separate my wants and needs?
I know for certain I can't control her
When together our talking is easy
I'd like to be tender — not push too much
The minute I do is when I'll lose her
The tug of desire makes me gutsy
She knows especially I want to touch.

She gave me two
of her knit hats
suffused with her
perfume — she knows
what she's doing.

There is no simpler method than doing
My wholehearted best while letting go of
Results especially with those whom I love
Because controlling them isn't loving
Imposing my will is self-defeating
Which I know from experience would shove
Them away from me when I want to move
Closer — simplicity is exhausting —
I want them to do what they want to do
They have perfect freedom to live their lives
Even if they choose to be without me
So the question becomes what do I do
When my thoughts are filled with self-doubting lies
When I am feeling ragged and empty?

I don't think I'm meant
to be comfortable and
indolent all the
time but I do need to learn
the art of relaxation.

Figuring out what I'm supposed to be
Doing is a question of making moves
And seeing what happens and I do shove
When I believe that it's necessary
To clarify an ambiguity
And I don't know what it is that I love
Unless I'm wholeheartedly a part of
The game of life with curiosity
Pushing up against my limitations
And seeing which it is that makes me — me —
Against difficulty disappointments
Being flexible with fluctuations
Seeking an intelligent repartee —
Because life questions and doesn't relent.

Am I doing life
or is life doing me?
There is provoking
repartee with love
and resonance.

I adore my chair and keyboard and the
Window that I look through in the morning
When I get to my desk — I love playing
With words and having them skip along a
Page easily and as lazy as a
Happy child — I like letting out a string
Of thought — I enjoy the job of coiling
The ends of lines with rhymes that may be a
Trick that a reader doesn't take the time
To notice — I look forward to the end
Of this poem — now I don't have a clue —
The momentum is building line to line —
I do hope this poem doesn't offend
My only goal is to entertain you.

What did you want?
Did you want something
Serious?

It's a pain that America depends
Upon the media's information
That's saturated with accusation
That makes it so difficult to defend
Disfavored views even among my friends
Mass opinion imposes force upon
Outsiders exerting the dominion
Of the nation's cleverest who pretend
To be civic-minded while instead it's
True they've mastered the art of accusing
Opponents of the very evils that
They themselves are guilty of and so it's
Good to be poised and not be the playthings
Of the propaganda of the autocrats.

Will we be ruled by
the cleverest and the most
ruthless among us
as propaganda is a
timeless tool of tyranny?

Accusation is a clever trick of
Misdirection as public attention
Focuses on the accused and not on
The accuser who is safely above
Suspicion because of the gimmick of
Hatred aroused by the circulation
Of slyly distorted information —
We need the strength of deeply rooted love
Of sincerity and integrity
That are precious qualities of the heart
Of courageous cultural warriors
Opposed to lies who then become lonely
Figures misunderstood and set apart
And targeted within the info-war.

For the innocent
and naïve the secrets and
inner workings of
society are almost
incomprehensible.

I do take a partisan point of view
I compose scorching editorials
Opposing hypocritical cabals
And over decades I've gotten used to
The taste of bitterness I attend to
But in my poems I don't want to brawl
I won't touch upon the issues at all
Because arguments divide me from you
Details of issues disappear with time
People are prone to bickering and war
I do a little to promote justice
It's a lot more fun to compose my rhymes
Partisan politics is just a bore
Poetry is my relaxing device.

Because I edit
an obscure little journal
of opinion I'm
not widely known or well paid
but I avoid the death threats.

It's a shame that more people cannot see
How America could be on the verge
Of losing so much as there is a surge
Of hatred that's dividing our country
With factions not bothering with mercy
With disapproved opinions being purged
And the death of free speech deserves a dirge
It's a pity to think how could it be
So many of our children are murdered
Not intentionally — by accident —
These kids are caught in the crossfire and shot
For media these deaths aren't worth a word
The gang violence is inconvenient
With expendable deaths — that's the upshot.

Kids who aren't being
justly educated and
are abandoned by
society don't add up
to political leverage.

Politics resembles psychodrama
And its personalities are brittle
The usual game is to belittle
Opponents with fabricated trauma
Concocted slanders depending on the
Lunatic factions sprinkling a spittle
I do my best to be noncommittal
Indifferent to the melodrama
But then the spectacle is sobering
Because politicians are serious
Apparently immune to feeling shame
While their narratives are mesmerizing
And their agendas are imperious
They are experts at utilizing blame.

Righteousness
turns opponents
into demons.

I do believe that there are honest men
And women of both parties who do their
Best to make decisions based on a fair
Reading of issues and we do depend
Upon courtesy and grace to befriend
All sorts of people who sincerely care
About decency and with whom we share
Our nation and with whom we may contend
And argue over the economy
On the difficult issues of justice
Working toward a peaceful coexistence
Supporting widely spread prosperity —
Revolutionaries are among us
American liberty needs defense.

Marxist ideology
pits classes and races
against each other
using hostility
to seize power.

Sincerity and integrity are
Ideals and liberty is a worthy
Cause and editorials are weighty
With thoughtful aggression designed to spar
And I've fabricated a repertoire
Of favorite views to push cleverly
But arguing doesn't make me happy
Accumulated bitterness leaves scars
It's true that warriors serve a purpose
They sacrifice their lives for a mission
Taking comfort in sister/brotherhood
We have a cherished legacy to lose
There is *esprit-de-corps* to draw upon
And yet I could forget it all for good.

Do opposing
warriors mirror
each other in
sincerity and
integrity?

Thic Nhat Hanh

A peace activist poet and teacher
A lovely Buddhist Vietnamese monk
Has died in Plum Village taking a chunk
From my heart to lose such a world leader
Such an open-hearted peaceful seeker
Of harmony who through his life debunks
Animosity by example junks
Partisanship and with compassion pours
Out his wisdom with loving-kindness
Bringing sunshine to unhappy people
Offering non-attachment and non-fear
With trust and confidence and mindfulness
Interpenetration is natural —
I hunger for peace — he serves as a spur.

For his *stupa* he requested
These words:

I am not in here
I am not out there either
I may be found in
your way of breathing
your way of walking.

I don't give myself to anything else
While slicing an orange and an apple
I allow my attention to be full
Of how the tips of my fingers hold the
Fruit with one of my hands — and of how the
Other guides the knife and keeps it stable —
The oranges are unpredictable —
Is it going to be a juicy or a
Dry orange? The knife goes through the apple
With just a tiny tug of resistance —
It's my habit to make quarter sections
And then to remove the inedible
Stem and the seeds to suit my preference
And there isn't any more to dwell on.

Anticipation
accompanies the
operation — will
the orange be sweet and
the apple honeyed?

This moment can be a seed of joy if
I follow what a crow is doing on
A branch and I notice it's bobbing on
One of the upper branches just as if
It's claiming a prominent perch as if
It's exerting a dominance upon
This little territory whereupon
It's bobbing and it's cawing in a riff
Of abrasive assaultive utterance
While I don't see any other bird or
Squirrels in the surrounding trees or on
The ground as it's casting a wary glance
Around — I don't know what is cawing for
And can't imagine what it's set upon.

Whatever the crow
was doing is beyond my
knowing as the world
is mysterious and now
the crow has moved somewhere else.

What can one say about the public schools
In Baltimore that fail to educate
Where even though the students graduate
They can't read and so they face a brutal
Existence guaranteed to have trouble
And yes I could have written boilerplate
Writing paragraphs that articulate
Who are the shamefully negligent fools
Responsible for the failing schools but
I don't have a clue about what to do
With the interlocked pattern of failure —
I think that fatherlessness is somewhat
To blame along with bureaucracy too
But there's so much heartache in Baltimore.

I only wrote the word
"Baltimore" once along
with Chicago and
New York as examples of
cities with gang violence.

In January in Baltimore there
Were 36 homicides and the
Police appear demoralized and the
Streets are controlled by the gangs who aren't scared
Of arrest because officials declared
That violations of law aren't worth the
Effort of prosecution prompting the
Casual sales of drugs in public squares
And that is just as well because the state's
Attorney is under indictment for
Financial shenanigans which is not
Surprising because we shouldn't fixate
On one lawyer — it's all happened before —
As public corruption is a blind spot.

Baltimore is in
Washington D.C.'s blind spot
even though it is
only 40 miles away
Baltimore doesn't make news.

The president's press secretary on
A Zoom meeting kibitzed about the news
Business being light-hearted and amused
That one provoking channel makes her yawn
Assuming these reporters are morons
Or are sleazy as they purposely skew
The facts by overemphasizing views
That are so foolishly dystopian —
They live in an alternate universe
She says defending her president and
Party denying the mayhem and fear
In big cities — she believes it's perverse
That correspondents have such freedom and
She thinks that this network is cavalier.

The video of
her Zoom comments was
broadcast by the
network that she dislikes —
she needs to be more careful.

Without a person looking into it
A mirror resembles an empty box
It becomes a curious paradox
There isn't an ounce of meaning to it
The open sky and the clouds don't need it
A mirror is also like a tinderbox
It depends upon a jack-in-the box
And needs an anxious person to use it
Without a conscious human being the
Mirror merely reflects and doesn't grow
Or influence the things about it but
Once it does reflect a person's face the
Mirror casts a spell and births an ego
Inside an image a person gets shut.

A mirror without
a face is like a box
without a lid.

There often wasn't very much to do
Standing in the outfield playing baseball
Just watching and waiting for a flyball
With teenage fantasies to follow through
With insecurity clouding my view
Playing my role and expecting fastballs
Doubting myself and anxious of curveballs
I had to be speedy to muddle through
Inning after inning I was waiting
I hungered for the chance to prove myself
But I was relieved when nothing happened
Being on edge and anticipating
I knew that a test would impose itself
Earning acceptance — that's what I wanted.

All the practice with
catching groundballs and flyballs
was part of growing
up and I'm remorseful of
the flying ball that jinxed me.

It's just a convention to play with rhymes
And I know the easily rhyming words
The sense of the poem can't be absurd
As logic should follow from line to line
I would like the meaning to be benign
It's propitious to write about birds
Inside this book flamingos are preferred
Their oddness and loveliness do combine
Usually I am not serious
It's nifty to confabulate rhythm
I'd like to end with a surprising joke
Being awkward is deleterious
Could you type by using only your thumbs?
My favorite plant is the artichoke.

The president is serious
Oh so sanctimonious
But he doesn't deign
To often explain
I think he is delirious.

Is there a more sublime image than a
Chubby boy playing a tuba puffing
His cheeks pursing his lips and vibrating
The air with a marvelous um-pa-pa
A low reverberating oom-ba-ba
A lovely metaphor symbolizing
A musical rendering of farting
And as a rascal I'd like to add a
Humble dollop by dropping an empty
Snail shell into the tuba picturing
The combination of curves within curves
A happy symmetry in sympathy
With a symphony of rhapsodizing
Frivolous phantasmagorical verve.

Do you think the
snail shell in the
lowermost curve
of the tuba
would rattle?

I close my eyes and listen intently
And absorb the sound inside the shell of
A conch a lovely epitome of
Nature's fantastic creativity
Frolicking with my receptivity
Rollicking with nonsensical thoughts of
An ear listening to the sound inside of
Another ear — is this a bumblebee?
The sighing and swelling of an ocean?
Or the sprinkling of rain upon a lake?
Is this the rhythm of my heart and blood?
The breaking of waves in lazy motion?
I may be giving myself a headache
With the commotion of a sprightly flood.

The absent conch
has left behind
a lovely pink ear
that I can hear.

How handy fingers are for typing these
Letters as the impulse of thought obtains
Expression tapping the keys to explain
This lovely quiet morning and to tease
Curiosity to see and to seize
Upon the barren branches that contain
A pink tinge of light that only remains
For a moment that diffuses and leaves
The trees in daylight — and how useful are
My hands that handle the panoply of
Forms of all the thousands of things I touch
Without really noticing that they are
Voluptuously tactile and I love
To caress the world — without thinking much.

My creased
fingers and palms
are a bridge to
phantasmagoria.

Every morning before the bathroom sink
I turn the faucet and the water runs
Scrubbing with a soapy liquid is fun
I splash my face and use the time to think
Suds get in my eyes and I have to blink
While shaving my face I do tend to hum
I scrape the razor and it does drag some
In the mirror I see my face is pink
My bathroom serves as a sanctuary
Inside the shower my thoughts are popping
Cascading water helps inspiration
I'm blissfully warm in February
Soap shampoo conditioner are flowing
In my head there's snappy fermentation.

Innocently bare
nakedly present
without defenses
I am who I am
and mostly happy.

Thirty-eight Years Ago . . .

I would leave home in the early evening
With no idea of where I would go
Whichever location I'd be solo
Constant loneliness was suffocating
The prospect of women was inviting
I was a dispirited Romeo
Whatever might happen I didn't know
The rush of my drinking was exciting
I hunted for fun with friendly strangers
And tried to forget my inhibitions
I had no clue of my perplexity
And rode a wave of possible danger
Big city avenues were a come-on
Wanting love is an addict's elegy.

Carousing on the
empty avenues of
big cities alone at
night looking for excitement
only led me to dead ends.

A hole in my soul had ahold of me
I was hurting but couldn't admit it
If you had asked I would have denied it
My own behavior was a mystery
I barely acknowledged my misery
I made a show of being a misfit
And pretended that I even liked it
I thought of myself as being gutsy
By getting used to feeling embarrassed
I didn't like cold sweats and hangovers
My head didn't clear until afternoon
My thinking capacity diminished
I prided myself on being clever
Others had problems — *but I was immune.*

My life narrowed to
a dark corridor
of closed doors but
I didn't notice.

At the detox center I say to the
Volunteers that I drink usually
On the weekends and occasionally
I do smoke a little weed during the
Week but only as a way to take the
Pressure off and it is true certainly
If you had my problems you'd drink too — *see?*
I am not alcoholic — don't like the
Word but maybe I am dependent on
Drugs and alcohol to some extent — *and*
They say that dependence is another
Word for alcoholism — whereupon
I surrender all my arguments and
The burden of shame lifts from my shoulders.

I realized that
I wasn't a bad person
but I *had* this thing
alcoholism — that went
a way toward understanding.

"*If you had my problems you would drink too*"
I meant those words and thirty days later
In a halfway house and feeling better
I saw those words — *just as I said them too* —
Which was a happy case of *deja vu*
Beside a pool table on a poster
While playing a game with two New Yorkers
Inside a house many addicts passed through
Sharing the mission of getting sober
We talked to each other — we all got jobs —
Youthful desperate — *they were just like me* —
There was our dignity to recover
We didn't fool ourselves — *we faced long odds* —
Getting drunk or drugged is very easy.

How could addicts so
youthful with so much
life to live heap so
much trouble upon
themselves as to be
hopeless?

Something's broken in an addict's thinking
Whatever normal is — *we are not that* —
And it's a predicament to get at
We don't notice that we're isolating
And we're experts at manipulating
Turning our families into doormats
Being dishonest we get skillful at
To our loved ones this is disheartening
It's not intentional but it happens
We push our loved ones to a breaking point
And then they have to turn their backs on us
Sometimes we enter a fatal tailspin
Every addiction reaches an endpoint
Would the world be better off without us?

Near the end the addict
is a pathetic
combination of
confusion self-pity
and resentment.

It's a big deal to get an addict to
A corner where he wants to stop and the
Decision has to come from within the
Addict — there is nothing at all to do
Except to allow the addiction to
Continue inevitably to the
Point where the addict recognizes a
Breaking point — it's a bad idea to
Exert control or force on him or her
Because the addict can't be outsmarted
Or separated from the drug or drink
But the agony of addiction serves
Even though it seems to be coldhearted —
Through pain — *to change the way the addict thinks.*

Only too much pain
will bring about
the necessary
change of
heart.

Both of them at the detox center were
Crafty — they took the opportunity —
They got me talking and listened to me
The night before was a confusing blur
A half-remembered shameful drunken slur
I drove drunk — the police arrested me —
The volunteers were kind and talked to me
They asked if I wanted something better
And sidestepped my pride and didn't fight it
Suggested that things were going to get worse
They calmly discussed alcoholism
I was conflicted and admitted it
But I wasn't evil — wasn't perverse —
My world disintegrated — I was *numb*.

Alcoholics
know what to say
and how to say
it to cornered
alcoholics.

I admitted I was alcoholic
And a weight was lifted from my shoulders
I didn't know — *but I turned the corner*
My denials and defenses were thick
Kindness and understanding did the trick
It was helpful that I was hung over
The volunteers were patient and clever
I freely accepted that I was sick
Only after I admitted defeat
Could I finally grasp my misery
I was stubbornly scrappy every day
My excuses were full of self-deceit
I felt the anger but not self-pity
I had earned *a sobriety birthday.*

After talking to
the volunteers I
went to a cot
and slept like a
newborn baby.

Who could love you after what you have done?
After the hell that you have put them through?
Really what do you expect them to do?
The betrayal of love can't be undone
Yours was a devilish game of hit-and-run
Your lying stealing absence were taboo
Do you imagine that they still love you?
Loving a desperado isn't fun
Your predicament can't be fixed with words
Your apologies aren't good enough now
For the moment you have to let them go
You remember the things that you ignored
You'd like to be better but don't know how
You'd rather be numb than to feel so low.

The easy escape
from the unbearable weight
of remorse and guilt
gives the urge to drink or drug
a most demonic allure.

The first few days and months are critical
You can live usefully — *you're not alone* —
There's a better way — *you have to be shown* —
It's true you are a genuine oddball
You can never safely drink alcohol
What you need today is a buffer zone
And you don't have to suffer on your own
For *now* your thoughts are unreliable
Nothing is more important than these days
Drinking again is the same as *dying*
You are not alone — *you have loving friends* —
We gather such strength in our repartee
It is necessary to *stop lying*
So be honest with us and don't pretend.

You will never find
people who understand you
better than we do
as we share your impulses
and together we are strong.

Nobody comes to recovery on
The wings of victory and it's a good
Thing too because without a defeat *would*
You think over your denials and could
You let go of what you depended on?
So much of what you believed is a con
You played the role of willing victimhood
The world was against you from where you stood
You couldn't find the place where you belonged
Painful thinking was the fuel for drinking
You see the world with a lopsided view
It doesn't matter if you're right or wrong
It is self-pity that you are fighting
Your *ragged* anger isn't helping you.

What underlies
the abandoned urge
to drink other than the
wish to escape the way you
think the world is?

You are odd — *but you're not one of a kind* —
You can find us inside every city
Off the Baltic Coral or Greenland seas
You can connect with us at any time
There are plenty of meetings now online
Please don't allow yourself to be lonely
Our banter makes for the best company
In our rooms we leave our troubles behind
Life gets difficult in isolation
Sorrow is magnified by solitude
The police will hunt you after midnight
Attitudes change with communication
I don't see the world the way that I did
I breathe freely and flourish in sunlight.

Sobriety turns
wretched experience
into useful and even
lighthearted
stories.

It's going to take some time to clear your head
Your body is polluted with toxins
You've gotten used to abnormal rhythms
As often as possible you've been wired
When coming down you are *so very tired*
Excitement brings fantastic illusions
Then they flip to horrific delusions
You've put effort into getting *wasted*
What will life be like without chemicals?
Thinking about the future causes dread
There are so many things you've avoided
You think that starting over is futile
It would be better to get high instead
You know that your thoughts are convoluted.

The idea of
facing existence without
the comforting shield
of intoxication is
almost paralyzing.

You have thought you may be cheating yourself
You do wonder if you are really good
You'd like to live decently if you could
And you've prided yourself on being tough
Of all this misery — *you've had enough* —
If you could live without the pain you would
If there were a better way then you should
But it's true that you barely trust yourself
Taking a drug or a drink is easy
Like lightning — *in an instant* — it's *over*
It's *so* familiar to have failed again
You do wonder if you're just *too* lazy
When the urge *bites* you are a pushover
There is a strange comfort inside the pain.

The morning after
with a splitting head and a
sweating body you
think there's no way you're going to
do it again — *but you do.*

The urge comes suddenly and you submit
Getting high amid a neon aura
Hunting for moments of euphoria
What is authentic? What is counterfeit?
An addict does become a hypocrite
With a drug-induced schizophrenia
With a despairing sense of inertia
But a part of you is longing to quit
You get to know the names of policemen
You do receive their hospitality
You make appointments to speak with judges
You ape the role of a comedian
You're missing the taste of reality
Your life has become a depressing trudge.

Everyone you know
drinks and drugs like you do —
you don't have a
problem — you just need to be
a little more careful.

An arrest an accident a divorce
Are activities to look forward to
You know catastrophe is overdue
The urge to drug is a devilish force
It overwhelms the anguish of remorse
The nagging guilt and shame are biting you
You don't have a hint about what to do
You're not improving *but are getting worse*
You are aware of being a time bomb
You finally admit that you are *done*
Just how you will live you don't have a clue
Reaching the end is called *hitting bottom*
This is not victory — *it is not fun* —
You are a regretful mess of a stew.

When I admitted —
I am an alcoholic
and a drug addict —
a weight was lifted from my
shoulders and I felt relief.

Each of us will take a turn in speaking
We go around the room telling stories
We will talk about what we did *with ease*
Don't be surprised if you hear us laughing
Your company today is inspiring
We know every detail of your *dis*ease
Have suffered *splendidly* for expertise
We know what it's like to be despairing
We each *hit bottom* to come in the door
From your perspective nothing is funny
We are cheerful and happy to meet you
Ours is a fellowship of simple rapport
We *were just like you* but now we are *free*
Our lives gain such *meaning* by helping you.

Your presence in the
circle — *so raw and exposed* —
reminds each of us
of the absolute anguish
of those first slippery days.

You are happy because you've let it go
You've admitted you can't live as you did
If you try you will probably be dead —
You thought you could manage — *you let it go* —
You thought you were special — *you let it go* —
You ignored your misery and your dread
You made a big fool of yourself instead
Those years of denial — *you've let them go* —
You didn't know how hard you were fighting
Until the very moment you gave up
And weight came off your shoulders — *you relaxed* —
There is no reason to keep on lying
For decades the pressure was building up
And then in an instant it all collapsed.

All those years
of misery
led to a moment
of release that changed
nothing but your attitude.

There are facts about *you* you may not know
You had very little power to choose
You had turned into a slave of the booze
When the urge came on you couldn't say no
Alcohol and drugs are devilish foes
If you think you control them *you're* confused
They determined you — you hadn't a clue
Your guardian angels were a no-show
There once was an alcoholic who drove
From Minnesota to Las Vegas and
Back in a blackout and he returned to
Precarious consciousness inside of
A hospital psych ward in St. Paul — and
The gas receipts explained where he'd been to.

There will come a time
and a place where no human
power can save you
from the urge to drink — only
a *Higher Power* does that.

You can choose your own idea of God
God is inside you — *you may not know it* —
God is present — *you may not believe it* —
You may think that God is wickedly flawed
Perhaps the churches are empty facades
And the preachers' sermons are counterfeit
You've fought like a devil not to submit
You're defiant of phony demagogues —
Can you see that defiance gets in the
Way of reliance and that you've put up
Barricades — and we are not asking you
To submit but to find an idea
Of a Higher Power that will show up
When no other human touch can save you?

Certainty is not
necessary — you
only need to
sincerely seek.

Those first few days and months are difficult
There are times of genuine happiness
When having friends is a new kind of bliss
But then your emotions are *virulent*
Your nagging impulses are dissonant
Fear and self-pity make for crankiness
Envy and resentment lead to nastiness
Stubbornness renders you ambivalent
For the first time you're feeling emotions
When over years addiction made you *numb*
You do encounter the fuel of your fire
Your mind simmers with painful explosions
You are deathly afraid of days to come
But you resolve not to remain a liar.

Newly sober
you are like a turtle
who has lost its shell
to find that its skin is
exquisitely sensitive.

There are no barriers into our groups
Happily we are not strangers to you
All these tribulations — *we've felt them too* —
We know the emotions that make you droop
We share experience that made you stoop
There are practices that will pull you through
We survive and prosper — *so you can too* —
Think of all the burdens that you will drop
We do suggest that you choose one of us
Together you will learn our principles
And disperse the terror of your secrets
And relearn the gift of innocent trust
You can regain your courteous scruples
And make propitious use of your wits.

Among us you will find
survivor's euphoria
rascality gratitude
uncommon honesty
and hilarious stories.

Hang on to the moment you surrendered
The turning point when you became *willing*
It was either that or keep on dying
At a lonely abyss your mind opened
And a glimmer of hope reawakened
Cosmic circumstances were aligning
And infinite forces were conspiring
Do you really comprehend what happened?
You didn't lose before an enemy
You finally quit a hopeless battle
And just stopped being stupidly stubborn
You gave yourself the gift of clemency
The lesson here is unforgettable
Upon this foundation new life is born.

Relaxation amid
difficult circumstances
is the most precious
gift.

You needn't define your Higher Power
But you should admit that *you are not it*
Whatever *it* is — *just stop fighting it* —
For years your Higher Power was liquor
You gave chemicals all of your power
You consecrated the drugs with your habits
You honored sacraments with your vomit
The taste of your life was toxic and sour
You need to believe in something to live
Some kind of succoring beneficence
Churches temples and synagogues could do
You need something worthy to stay alive
Gather the power of good common sense
Come to believe this power is *in* you.

If you have trouble
believing in a Higher
Power for now just
suppose it *might* exist and
that it *could* help you to live.

No one can transfer this power to you
You can only find it *within* yourself
Perhaps you'll see that it grows *of itself*
It can provide such confidence to you
You'll gain integrity and knowledge too
You don't need to solve problems by yourself
As so many troubles will solve themselves
You may find the answers will come to you
The trick is *reliance — not defiance —*
You'll want to turn your life over to *it*
This undefinable something guides you
It's much better than your self-reliance
So good intentions and behavior fit
You will find the cosmos supporting you.

Having good intentions
giving your best efforts
while turning over
results to a Higher Power
summon relaxation.

People will ask me after 38
Years why I keep going to my meetings
Won't I ever be congratulating
Myself on being good and living straight
After so many decades why fixate
On memories that should be receding
As I've earned my sanity by proving
Myself recovered sharing not a trait
Of those desperadoes? But they don't know
I could easily become an addict
Again as our years of experience
Show that none of us is safe — time winnows
Us — *it is impossible to predict*
Who will fall — sobriety is a dance.

Because the pattern
of addiction lives in me
I can't afford to
indulge the attitudes that
are tinder to the burning.

Besides I've gotten used to a level
Of friendship and communication that
Is rarely found outside of our groups that
Is premised on honesty and good will
That out of our suffering we distill
The commonsensical principles that
Will defuse an exasperation that
Tempts me to burn it all to hell until
Nothing but ashes remains — *so you see* —
The devil is still inside of me and
Although I appear to be sensible
I do like my tinge of rascality
That does balance my integrity and
Renders me especially lovable.

You could say that a
recovered alcoholic
and addict may be
many things but certainly
not a predictable bore.

Edward Scissorhands

In a movie Edward Scissorhands is
A sweet creation of an inventor
Who died leaving no one to look after
Edward who's abandoned and left on his
Own in a mansion on a hill which is
Sad as Edward couldn't be lonelier
Edward is pure and couldn't be nicer —
It is a predicament that Edward is
Not finished as his creator didn't
Have the time to make for Edward *proper*
Human hands so he languishes alone
In a spooky manor and he doesn't
Have the occasion to receive and share
Genuine love — *Edward needs to be shown.*

Instead of having
the *soft palms and fingertips*
we take for granted
Edward possesses wires
and the sharpest of steel blades.

Then a woman named Peg who's an Avon
Lady selling cosmetics is having
Difficulty because she's not making
Sales so she ascends the hill and comes upon
The dusty empty mansion whereupon
She sees Edward in the dark cowering
In a corner — *and Edward is trembling* —
Doesn't know what to do — being withdrawn
Within himself for so long and meeting
Peg so suddenly is confusing and
Peg is taken aback by his scissor-
Hands but Peg is kindly considering
His forlorn abandoned existence and
His oddly benevolent demeanor.

Peg Boggs decides to
take Edward from the mansion
down the hill in her
car to live with the Boggs
in their *domicile* in town.

Edward's scissors are *multitudinous*
The many blades on each of his hands makes
Adapting to life difficult — it takes
Thoughtful effort to button a shirt — *plus* —
He's never had a comb — his hair's a mess —
So it's not strange that he suffers outbreaks
Of anxiety with throbbing headaches
But Peg expresses a feminine fuss
She shows him the marvels of a mirror
She provides him a sense of normalcy
He compares himself with everyone else
With a shock he perceives that he is weird
He's made aware of his deformity
He knows that he looks like nobody else.

Edward has the most
difficulty balancing
successfully a
pea upon a blade of a
scissor while eating supper.

Peg has a teenage daughter who is Kim
Is Edward attracted to her? *Sort of*
Does Kim suppose that he is odd? *Kind of*
Kim has never seen a person like him
Dangling razor-sharp mechanical limbs
Days before he couldn't conceive of *love*
Edward doesn't know what he's dreaming of
A captivating hypnotizing *whim*
He notices a *pang* in his stomach
He hasn't a clue about what to do
These new sensations only confuse him
Overwhelming longing that makes him *ache*
It's an exhilarating rendezvous
Poor Edward can't stop thinking about *Kim*.

Kim has a boyfriend
named *Jim* who smirks and jokes
about Edward's plight
balancing and dropping peas
at the family supper.

In town the women are interested
About this mysterious character
They speculate why Peg would sequester
The waif within her home separated
Suspiciously perhaps to be confined
And selfishly enjoyed which is *bizarre*
So that the frustrated ladies *concur*
It's proper that Edward be presented
To society and celebrated
And thereupon the women converge at
Peg's front door and they insist that she host
A barbecue for him to be *revealed*
So that everyone could mingle and chat
Where they will bring salads — with which to *boast*.

Joyce Monroe
insistently feeds
spoonfuls of her
ambrosia salad to
a confused Edward.

Even with the self-inflicted scars on
His face Edward is a handsome young man
And innocent too as the women can
Tell — *what erotica to come upon —*
What curiosity that Edward spawns —
They've never seen such unusual hands
Which do so much to stimulate their glands
His complexion is intriguingly wan
Edward has skillfully trimmed the hedges
About the yard and shown himself to be
An expert sculptor creating perfect
Statues of the Boggs family with his
Blades — it's obvious he is a marquee
Artist — captivating in all respects.

The ladies of the town
line up to have Edward
cut their hair in the
most *exotic* styles.

In addition to cutting women's hair
Edward trims poodles and shih tzus also
Women implore him — he doesn't say no —
He is innocent — why *should* he beware?
Celebrity is a happy affair
While he is shy his reputation grows
He appears on a variety show
Edward's vulnerable and not aware
He is pushed to open a hair salon
He's brought to a bank to secure a loan
With no Social Security number
Without any credit to draw upon
His employment history is unknown
They do ask him to try again later.

Joyce Monroe
leads Edward to the
back room of a proffered
salon *where she disrobes*
and *Edward runs away.*

On returning home Kim and Jim were locked
Out of the house and Edward unlocked the
Door with a little blade which gave Jim a
Nefarious and *sneaky* scheme that shocked
Kim — who really dislikes the way Jim mocks
Edward — Jim pushed Edward to unlock a
Door inside his Dad's house that leads to a
Guarded chamber and so Jim *concocted*
A plan and *bullied* Kim and Edward to
Break into the room and to burglarize
Money while his Dad was on vacation —
For the caper they dressed in black to do
The deed while Kim was unhappy and seized
With doubt and *dreadful anticipations*.

Jim was outsmarted by
an alarm that summoned the
the Police — Jim and Kim
escaped — *but Edward was
arrested.*

Edward's hands do look like lethal weapons
Edward was lucky that he wasn't shot
The police were nervous when he was caught
Those first moments were critical seconds
They were poised to shoot a barrage of rounds
"*Drop your weapons*" they said but he could not
Poor Edward was twisted in mental knots
He did his best to follow directions
Then the neighborhood ladies intervened
They got the police to lower their guns
And Edward was cuffed and taken to jail
He stayed overnight and then he was freed
Because the judge believed he wouldn't run
Peg and her husband Bill put up the bail.

The judge treated him
with leniency because
a psychologist
deemed Edward to be without
knowledge of *proper morals*.

From the beginning Kim was standoffish
All she could see was that Edward was odd
Tongue-tied and awkward and horribly *clawed*
But she notices that Jim is selfish
He's greedy dishonest and devilish
She's disgusted with his phony façade
She thinks that Jim's love for her is a fraud
Edward's entrapment is not what she wished
Kim is embarrassed in Edward's presence
She feels so ashamed and also guilty
Edward's in trouble — *so what can she do?*
Edward embodies innocent patience
Why did Edward come? Why did he agree?
Edward said because she wanted him to.

Kim is the only
one who sees the injustice of
Edward's circumstance
from a comprehending and
an *adoring* point of view.

Peg's husband Bill has a talk with Edward
While the family is having supper
He asks Edward which he thinks is better
With found money — would he give it to friends?
Would he claim it as his own and pretend?
The police would take it — *if he prefers*
Which course of action is really proper?
Edward's confused — *he doesn't understand* —
Saying he'd give it to *his family*
Bill and Peg are *disappointed* with him
Going to the police was the answer
They correct Edward but do it *gently*
They're unhappy to see him sad and *grim*
Edward's inarticulate — *he stutters.*

They assume Edward
attempted burglary to
obtain the money
to open the hair salon —
they think he's ignorant.

The ladies in town are doubting Edward
Joyce suggests that there's something wrong with him
And Joyce is afraid for Peg's daughter Kim
Edward has earned a criminal record
His raunchy behavior can't be ignored
In spite of his talent he may be dim
Prospects for honest redemption are slim
Joyce admits that she's frightened of Edward
At the salon *Edward accosted her*
Edward attempted to remove her clothes
Thank goodness she *escaped* and wasn't *raped*
Edward isn't shy — *he's an imposter* —
What he's capable of *only God knows*
His genuine nature is taking shape.

Among themselves the
ladies agree that Peg and
Bill are blameless but
they decide not to go to
Peg's yearly Christmas party.

Edward is lonely and disconsolate
Jim is furious and has threatened him
Jim has warned him to stay away from Kim
It is hard for Edward to concentrate
Edward turns to sculpture to compensate
Carving a large ice angel pleases him
It is true the angel resembles Kim
Like snow the ice crystals accumulate
Edward is absorbed and lost in his work
He doesn't know that Kim is watching him
Kim is moved and dances within the snow
Kim is *enraptured* with Edward's artwork
Her attitude has changed — *now she loves him* —
She *does adore* him — *but he doesn't know.*

With a sweeping flick
of a blade Edward inflicts
an *inadvertent*
slice into Kim's upreaching
palm — *as Jim has slyly seen.*

Jim exclaimed "Get the hell out of here — *freak* —
You can't touch anything without destroying
It completely — and if you're not leaving
Now then I am going to *kill you* — *you geek*"
Peg came on the scene — got scared — and she s*hrieked*
She saw Edward frightened and Kim bleeding
She took Kim inside — Edward was fleeing —
Edward felt so very shameful and weak
He hated himself — *which made him angry* —
And Edward ran without a place to go
And punctured the tires of cars on the way
The neighbors saw him — *Edward was scary* —
They saw that Edward was a tornado
Of swirling knives — *and today was doomsday.*

On Christmas Eve
the night of Peg's party
the neighbors called the police
to hunt for Edward who had
become a *maniac*.

Peg is sorry thinking about Edward
She realized she hadn't thought it through
Of what bringing him home could *really* do
To themselves — to the town — and to Edward —
She is upset regretful — *and she's scared* —
So much happened that she'd like to undo
The whole society has come unglued
But at the moment just where is Edward?
Thankfully it's true — Kim's not deeply cut —
She is only scratched slightly — *where's Edward?* —
She and Bill decide to drive and find him
They need to act before someone gets hurt
Both Bill and Peg are nervous and afraid
Edward's not safe — *they need to protect him.*

Peg thinks that after
all maybe it's better that
Edward return to
the mansion on the hill so
things could return to normal.

Edward's anger dissipated quickly
He meandered in a circular way
There wasn't any place to run away
He kept within the shadows stealthily
He returned to the Boggs' home quietly
Edward calmly bore his *naiveté*
He encountered Kim inside the doorway
She welcomed him apologetically
And Kim wanted Edward to embrace her
And Edward wholeheartedly longed to
But Edward Scissorhands whispered "I can't"
He knew he couldn't without hurting her
Once again — *he didn't know what to do* —
He could only repeat himself — *"I can't."*

Kim wasn't so
easily dissuaded
from her expression
of affection — she
embraced Edward.

Jim was driving and hunting for Edward
He was crazy and drinking heavily
He was furious and drove stupidly
Kim's brother Kevin visited a friend
It was late and he was walking homeward
Kevin was tired and walked unconsciously
Jim was drunk and swerving dangerously
Edward saw them both — *and so it happened* —
Edward rushed to the scene and then he lunged
He knocked Kevin safely out of the way
Jim barely missed them — *he screeched to a stop* —
Edward and Kevin became excited
And both of their arms were flailing away
The neighbors were watching and called the cops.

To the neighbors
it seemed that Edward
was attacking and
cutting Kevin
with whirling blades.

Edward Scissorhands is a poor fellow
He can't touch people as he would like to
And he's perplexed about what he *can do*
The scene on the street was a wild tableau
A swarming mob became a volcano
Jim jumped on Edward and a fight ensued
Edward defended himself — *his arms corkscrewed* —
Jim was sliced and slashed and so he bellowed
Peg and Bill arrived and rescued Kevin
People swarmed on Edward and they got cut
Edward got to his feet — *began to run* —
The empty mansion was his direction
Edward was appalled and knew in his gut
What had happened could never be undone.

A police cruiser
followed Edward
to the gates of
the mansion and
four shots were heard.

The boiling mob on the street followed on
Kim checked on Kevin and came along too
She was scared about what the mob would do
Housewives and husbands were running along
They were shouting howling coming on
Such a commotion on the avenue
Kim came to the gate and she ran on through
What happened to Edward — *where had he gone?*
"It's over it's over so please go home"
The policeman yelled — *and then he drove away* —
The crowd was angry and dissatisfied
They were enraged — *no one was going home* —
They were frustrated *crazed* and hunting *prey*
Edward's a monster and *must* be finished.

The iron gate to
the mansion on the
hill was down on the
ground and the road
wound upwards.

Kim came to the mansion and saw the grounds
There was a garden — and sculpted hedges —
And there were flowers along the edges
She entered the mansion and then she found
A broad stepped staircase and upward she bound
In the highest chamber — there Edward was —
She believed he was killed but *here* he was
She cried with relief — *wound her arms around
Him* — Edward was frightened — *out of his head* —
Only for moments the lovers embraced
She told him Kevin was really OK
She was so sorry — *she loved him* — she said
But just for mere seconds could she embrace
Him — on this *beastly cataclysmic* day.

Jim bolted in
the room holding
a gun — he aimed
and shot at Edward
but missed.

A part of the roof caved in upon Jim
He was startled and let go of the gun
Edward knelt down and he looked to be stunned
Jim seized a beam and savagely beat him
Jim was obsessed and forgot about Kim
He was determined — *had only begun* —
Kim would never forgive what he had done
She took an iron poker and hit him
Jim turned upon Kim and he knocked her down
Edward stood up and pressed blades to his chest
Edward pushed forward and the blades went through
Jim fell from a window — *dead on the ground* —
The mob was approaching — *Kim couldn't rest* —
She said *goodbye* — as she was *forced* to do.

Kim grabbed some scraps
of blades hung
on a rack — she
ran down the stairs
and out the door.

Then Kim confronted the mob at the door
She told them that Edward and Jim were dead
They battled and killed each other she said
No one in there is alive anymore
They could see for themselves — *just through the door* —
"You can see these blades for yourselves" she said
The crowd dispersed and went home instead
They thought they had got what they lusted for
Kim decided to go — *to leave Edward* —
She knew that he couldn't be safe in town —
Many years have passed — Edward lives alone —
Kim is full of remorse about Edward
He is protected and shouldn't come down
She's sorry he has to live on his own.

Her eyes often
return to the
mansion on the
hill especially
on Christmas Eve.

Too woo
women

is to
play

and sus-
pend

the
moment —

one

doesn't

hold

control.

Only banana

tastes like banana

only a tongue

can taste banana —

I have the joy.

—*Tekkan*

www.ingramcontent.com/pod-product-compliance
Lightning Source LLC
Chambersburg PA
CBHW040419100526
44589CB00021B/2753